WITHDRAWN

REGENTS RENAISSANCE DRAMA SERIES 176

General Editor: Cyrus Hoy
Advisory Editor: G. E. Bentley

THE GENTLEMAN USHER

GEORGE CHAPMAN

The Gentleman Usher

Edited by

JOHN HAZEL SMITH

UNIVERSITY OF NEBRASKA PRESS · LINCOLN

MANUFACTURED IN THE UNITED STATES OF AMERICA

Regents Renaissance Drama Series

The purpose of the Regents Renaissance Drama Series is to provide soundly edited texts, in modern spelling, of the more significant plays of the Elizabethan, Jacobean, and Caroline theater. Each text in the series is based on a fresh collation of all sixteenth- and seventeenth-century editions. The textual notes, which appear above the line at the bottom of each page, record all substantive departures from the edition used as the copy-text. Variant substantive readings among sixteenth- and seventeenth-century editions are listed there as well. In cases where two or more of the old editions present widely divergent readings, a list of substantive variants in editions through the seventeenth century is given in an appendix. Editions after 1700 are referred to in the textual notes only when an emendation originating in some one of them is received into the text. Variants of accidentals (spelling, punctuation, capitalization) are not recorded in the notes. Contracted forms of characters' names are silently expanded in speech prefixes and stage directions, and, in the case of speech prefixes, are regularized. Additions to the stage directions of the copy-text are enclosed in brackets. Stage directions such as "within" or "aside" are enclosed in parentheses when they occur in the copy-text.

Spelling has been modernized along consciously conservative lines. "Murther" has become "murder," and "burthen," "burden," but within the limits of a modernized text, and with the following exceptions, the linguistic quality of the original has been carefully preserved. The variety of contracted forms (*'em, 'am, 'm, 'um, 'hem*) used in the drama of the period for the pronoun *them* are here regularly given as *'em*, and the alternation between *a'th'* and *o'th'* (for *on* or *of the*) is regularly reproduced as *o'th'*. The copy-text distinction between preterite endings in *-d* and *-ed* is preserved except where the elision of *e* occurs in the penultimate syllable; in such cases, the final syllable is contracted. Thus, where the old editions read "threat'ned," those of the present series read "threaten'd." Where, in the old editions, a contracted preterite in *-y'd* would yield *-i'd* in modern spelling (as in "try'd," "cry'd," "deny'd"), the word is here given in its full form (e.g., "tried," "cried," "denied").

Punctuation has been brought into accord with modern practices. The effort here has been to achieve a balance between the generally light pointing of the old editions, and a system of punctuation which, without overloading the text with exclamation marks, semicolons, and dashes, will make the often loosely flowing verse (and prose) of the original syntactically intelligible to the modern reader. Dashes are regularly used only to indicate interrupted speeches, or shifts of address within a single speech.

Explanatory notes, chiefly concerned with glossing obsolete words and phrases, are printed below the textual notes at the bottom of each page. References to stage directions in the notes follow the admirable system of the Revels editions, whereby stage directions are keyed, decimally, to the line of the text before or after which they occur. Thus, a note on 0.2 has reference to the second line of the stage direction at the beginning of the scene in question. A note on 115.1 has reference to the first line of the stage direction following line 115 of the text of the relevant scene.

CYRUS HOY

University of Rochester

Contents

List of Abbreviations

Abbott   E. A. Abbott. *A Shakespearian Grammar*. London, 1929.

Brereton   J. L. Brereton. Review of Parrott 1 (see below). *Modern Language Review*, III (1907–1908), 396–401.

corr.   corrected state

ess.   essentially

Florio   John Florio. *A Worlde of Wordes, Or Most copious, and exact Dictionarie in Italian and English*. London, 1598.

Linthicum   M. C. Linthicum. *Costume in the Drama of Shakespeare and His Contemporaries*. Oxford, 1936.

OED   *Oxford English Dictionary*

Parrott   T. M. Parrott, ed. *The Plays and Poems of George Chapman: The Comedies*. London, 1914. This often agrees with Parrott 1; Parrott's copy-text for this edition was Shepherd.

Parrott 1   T. M. Parrott, ed. *"All Fooles" and "The Gentleman Usher" By George Chapman*. The Belles-Lettres Series. Boston, 1907. The listing of a reading from Parrott 1 implies that Parrott has a different reading.

Partridge   Eric Partridge. *Shakespeare's Bawdy*. London, 1947.

Q   Quarto of 1606

S.D.   stage direction

Shepherd   R. H. Shepherd, ed. *The Works of Chapman: Plays*. London, 1874.

Smith   Irwin Smith. *Shakespeare's Blackfriars Playhouse: Its History and Design*. New York, 1964.

S.P.   speech prefix

Sugden   A. H. Sugden. *A Topographical Dictionary to the Works of Shakespeare and His Fellow Dramatists*. Publications of the University of Manchester, No. 168. Manchester, 1925.

Tilley   M. P. Tilley. *A Dictionary of the Proverbs in England in the Sixteenth and Seventeenth Centuries*. Ann Arbor, 1950.

uncorr.   uncorrected state

Yamada   Akihiro Yamada. "An Edition of George Chapman's 'The Gentleman Vsher'." M.A. thesis, Shakespeare Institute, University of Birmingham, 1962. (Many of Yamada's readings are printed in his "Emendations in *The Gentleman Usher* [1606]," *Journal of the Faculty of Arts, Shinshu University*, No. 1 [Dec., 1966], 19–26.)

Introduction

TEXT

What is almost certainly Chapman's *The Gentleman Usher* was entered in the Stationers' Register on November 26, 1605, as the copyright of Valentine Simmes: "Entred for his copy vnder the handes of m^r harsenet and the Wardens A book called Vincentio & Margaret."[1] In due course the play was printed in a quarto under its present title: "The Gentleman Vsher. By George Chapman. At London Printed by V. S. for Thomas Thorppe. 1606." Evidently Simmes, the printer, had transferred ownership of the copyright to Thorpe, the publisher, but there is nothing particularly unusual in this known history of the play's publication. The quarto, the only known printing until the late nineteenth century, is perforce the copy-text of any modern edition.[2]

The quarto was probably printed from the author's manuscript: judging from the cleanness of the text, very likely a fair copy. A prompter's manuscript would surely not have lacked speech prefixes as the quarto does at I.ii.11 and II.i.215, or have had such vague speech assignments as those at II.i.159–168, or have misassigned to a character not on stage the speech at IV.iv.25; but an author composing (or copying) in haste could have made such mistakes.[3] Similarly, the omission of important names from an entry (III.ii.

---

1 W. W. Greg, *A Bibliography of the English Printed Drama to the Restoration*, I (London, 1939), 21. Harsnet was the licenser of books. For a bibliographical description of the quarto, see Greg, I, §226.

2 W. C. Hazlitt claimed that an "early MS. copy" under the title *The Will of a Woman* was sold among Richard Heber's books (*A Manual for the Collector and Amateur of Old English Plays* [London, 1892], p. 94). The title could be reasonably applied to *The Gentleman Usher*, but Greg found no listing of it in the sale catalogues (E. K. Chambers, *The Elizabethan Stage*, III [Oxford, 1923], 253). Hazlitt's statement must be a confusion of some sort. The catalogues (*Bibliotheca Heberiana* [London, 1834–1836]) do list three copies of the 1606 quarto.

3 The omitted speech prefixes could have been overlooked by the compositor; the abnormal position, without indentation, of the speech prefix at IV.iv.25 raises the possibility that it was added during a press correction.

229.1–3); an entry for an *ancilla* who plays no part in the scene (V.ii. 0.1); a number of vague entries, "others" and "&c." (I.ii.48.2, II.i.179.3, IV.i.10.1, etc.); and the placement at III.ii.282 and 297 of stage directions describing action which *has been* occurring all suggest an author's mind, not the more precise requirements of a promptbook. The Latin stage directions at V.i.49 and 53 could be Chapman's. It is just possible that the manuscript had received some preliminary markings from a prompter: *"Strozza following close"* (II.i.0.1) could be, as Parrott thought, a prompter's warning to an actor who must enter a little later; and some stage directions contain words which appear to be late additions, conceivably by a prompter (III.ii.229.2, *"Lasso"*; IV.v.0.1, *"Bassiolo going before"*; V.iv.39.2, *"Strozza before"*). But most or all of these traits could as easily be authorial; so could the erroneous reference given in V.iii.33, whether or not it is, as Parrott thought, a marginal note that was incorporated into the text by mistake.[4]

On the whole, the quarto is very well printed. Large portions of it, at least, were carefully proofread, for there are more than one hundred press corrections. I have collated copies (some in reproduction) from the University of Illinois, Harvard, Boston Public Library, the University of Texas, British Museum (three copies), and Eton; I have also relied on Yamada's collation of eleven additional copies.[5] Eight formes exist in corrected and uncorrected states: A-outer, C-outer, E-inner, F-outer, H-outer (which also has a third state), H-inner, I-outer, and K-inner. Only a small number of the variants are substantive. The alterations of *Superintendent* to *Vsher* in C-outer (II.i.154 and 162), the addition of a line in I-outer (V.ii.82), and the dropping of words in E-inner (III.ii.276) seem unlikely to have been a compositor's sophistications of his text. They could be corrections

---

[4] T. M. Parrott, ed., *The Plays and Poems of George Chapman: The Comedies* (London, 1914), p. 769. Parrott thought (p. 753) that "the quarto was printed from a stage copy." My conclusion agrees substantially with those of W. T. Jewkes, *Act Division in Elizabethan and Jacobean Plays 1583–1616* (Hamden, Conn., 1958), p. 254; and of Akihiro Yamada, "Bibliographical Studies of George Chapman's *The Gentleman Usher* (1606) Printed by Valentine Simmes," *Shakespeare Studies* (Shakespeare Society of Japan), II (1963), 83–90. But Yamada argued that a few pages of the manuscript had been fouled by a major authorial revision, an argument which I find wholly unconvincing.

[5] Yamada, "Bibliographical Studies," pp. 91–96; there are several minor inaccuracies in Yamada's collations of the copies which I have examined.

of compositorial oversight caused by inadequately marked revisions in the manuscript, as could the addition of a stage direction in H-inner (V.i.40.1); the words in III.ii.276 could have been lost in a typographical accident.[6] But all these changes could be evidence that Chapman himself read proof and made some revisions in the process; so could the addition, in an already corrected forme (H-outer), of quotations marking a maxim-like couplet (V.ii.43–44). Several variants are corrections of obvious misprints, and a few are improvements of punctuation; but an amazing number of changes seem no more than fussy tinkering, and the compositor at times went to some trouble to effect them: e.g., changing a capital to a lower-case letter in one part of a line to make room for the trifling addition of a comma in another part. It is hard to imagine a compositor allowing a proofreading author to dictate troublesome changes of trivia in set type, but it is just as hard to imagine the compositor making the changes on his own authority. My textual notes record only a few of the press variants, but I have recorded some semi-substantive variants, especially when I have preferred the uncorrected reading.

After an intensive bibliographical analysis, Yamada made a strong case for his view that two compositors set the quarto from cast-off copy,[7] but the division of the work remains in doubt. Such textual problems as exist, then, must be resolved on other grounds. I have tended to resolve such problems more conservatively than Parrott did, following the quarto in several places where he emended (e.g., III.ii.248 and IV.iii.72) and preserving as prose some passages which he broke into verses.

DATE

The Gentleman Usher was surely written for a children's company: the large cast and especially the importance of music and dancing and the inclusion of masques are characteristic of children's plays. It is invariably assigned to the Children of the Chapel, who performed

---

6 If so, the words should be retained in my text; they fit metrically and show clearly Alphonso's change of address. But I have excluded them because they are unnecessary and, if written by Chapman, were perhaps deleted by him (in a manuscript which the compositor at first overlooked) to show that Vincentio's aloofness from the courtly group continues through-out Alphonso's stay on stage.

7 Yamada, "Bibliographical Studies," pp. 99–102.

under various names at Blackfriars from 1600 to 1608, but no records of performances, either during that period or later, have survived.

The child actors—boys impressed into service, sometimes ruthlessly impressed, at age eight or ten—competed very successfully with the adult companies by putting on weekly performances before sophisticated audiences which paid high admission prices to be entertained. The entertainment was often satirical of court and government and of current drama; the "little eyases," as they are petulantly called in *Hamlet*, mimicked and perhaps burlesqued the style of the professional men, and the children's plays regularly satirized materials in adult plays and in other children's plays.[8] C. W. Wallace may have overstated when he said that Chapman "took from Shakespeare materials or suggestions in every play he wrote for the Chapel Children,"[9] but he and others have offered appealing evidence that Bassiolo is a parody of Malvolio, the steward in Shakespeare's *Twelfth Night*, which is usually dated 1601. And there are some indications that Chapman at times had John Marston's *Antonio's Revenge* in mind; for instance, Marston's play, written for a rival children's company, Paul's Boys, about 1600, might have suggested the name *Strozza*, for one of its characters is Gaspar Strotzo.[10]

More explicitly allusive, but not necessarily satirical, is Bassiolo's scornful nickname, Sir Giles Goosecap, for one of Lasso's servants (II.i.81). This probably refers to the titular hero of an anonymous play, now universally regarded as Chapman's, published in 1606 but written earlier, probably between late 1601 and early 1603.[11] Parrott makes a good case for other relationships between *The Gentleman Usher* and *Sir Giles Goosecap*: Corteza's drunk scene (III.ii. 231–271) may originally have been plotted for Lady Furnifall in

---

[8] For an account of the children's companies, see Alfred Harbage, *Shakespeare and the Rival Tradition* (New York, 1952); and H. N. Hillebrand, *The Child Actors*, Illinois Studies in Language and Literature, XI (Urbana, 1926).

[9] Wallace, *The Children of the Chapel at Blackfriars, 1597–1603*, University Studies of the University of Nebraska, VIII (Lincoln, 1908), 167.

[10] See below, p. xix; for another striking resemblance of detail, see n. 20. The following parallels are also interesting, but not unique to these two plays: Balurdo's and Bassiolo's fascination with new words like *endear* (*Revenge*, II.i.46; *Usher*, III.ii.410); Balurdo's and Pogio's dreams (*Revenge*, I.ii.125; *Usher*, I.i.5, 38); Maria's and Strozza's sermons on wifely virtues (*Revenge*, I.i.46; *Usher*, V.ii.17). My references to *Antonio's Revenge* are to G. K. Hunter's edition, Regents Renaissance Drama Series (Lincoln, 1965).

[11] Parrott, *The Comedies,* p. 890.

Goosecap, Pogio's habit of reversing things is also a fault of Sir Giles, and the scene in which Bassiolo gives Vincentio's letter to Margaret and writes an answer (III.ii.315–507) has some similarities to *Goosecap*, IV.i.67–192.[12] Almost certainly *The Gentleman Usher* must postdate *Sir Giles Goosecap*, as well as *Twelfth Night* and *Antonio's Revenge*, but if some of the allusions are in fact satirical the difference in time was probably not too great or the satire would have lost its point. F. G. Fleay's date of late 1601 and Wallace's of the summer of 1601 seem a bit early;[13] I prefer Parrott's date of late 1602[14] or early 1603.[15] We may perhaps exclude everything later than May, 1603, when the theaters were closed because of a plague epidemic; they remained closed for almost a year. Although it is tempting to view Medice, the upstart nobleman, as satirizing the many noblemen elevated by James shortly after his accession to the English throne in 1603, we are probably safer in dating the play during the last months of Elizabeth's reign. It is certainly difficult to believe that Chapman would have written *The Gentleman Usher*, with its satirical portrait of the titular figure and its unfavorable treatment of several courtly types, after his own appointment as sewer in ordinary to Prince Henry (*c.* 1604). Nominally, the position of sewer (a sort of headwaiter) was so similar to that of a gentleman usher (see Appendix

12 T. M. Parrott, "The Authorship of 'Sir Gyles Goosecappe'," *Modern Philology*, IV (1906), 33–35.

13 Fleay, *A Biographical Chronicle of the English Drama 1559–1642*, I (London, 1891), 58; Wallace, p. 75. Incidentally, Hazlitt dated the play which he called *The Will of a Woman* 1598 (see *n.* 2).

14 *The Comedies*, p. 753. Chambers (III, 251) accepts Parrott's date as "plausible enough," but thinks 1604 "also possible."

15 It is barely possible that Chapman alludes at II.i.253–255 to William Fowldes' translation of the pseudo-Homeric *Batrachomyomachia*, published sometime in 1603; see my note to those lines. Also conceivable is that one or two details in the play were influenced by the case of Agnes Howe, which Chapman used in his lost play *The Old Joiner of Aldgate* and which consequently brought Chapman into legal troubles in May, 1603 (C. J. Sisson, *Lost Plays of Shakespeare's Age* [Cambridge, 1936], pp. 12–79). The events in that case began in 1600, but Chapman finished his play about them "presently after christmas," 1602, and presumably had learned of them not much earlier. The case, a complicated one involving an heiress and rival suitors, is not fundamentally similar to the plot of *The Gentleman Usher*, but as described later in court proceedings it included a ritual marriage contract remotely similar to that between Vincentio and Margaret (Sisson, p. 28) and a threat by the heroine to kill herself in several ways which might have suggested Margaret's thoughts in V.iii (Sisson, pp. 35, 38).

C) that the play would have invited discomforting comparisons between its characters and figures in James' court.

There are several parallels between *The Gentleman Usher* and Marston's *Malcontent*. Maquerelle, the "old pand'ress" of Marston's play, has much in common with the "lusty widow" Corteza, and her sermon on the importance of physical beauty (II.iv.35) could serve as a burlesque of the Platonic discussion of beauty in *Usher*, IV.v. The name of Marston's villain, "Mendoza," might be related to "Mendice," true name of the fraudulent nobleman Medice, and the two men are similar in some ways: Mendoza is made a duke by Aurelia, who boasts (II.v.79) that she is a Medici; both Mendoza and Medice plot murders which fail; and both are finally driven from the stage as unworthy of being killed. The ignorance of a character is shown at one point in each play by an identical technique: Pogio says "Nassus" for "Parnassus" (I.i.33) and Mendoza says "Gisthus" for "Aegisthus" (I.v.9). Although the anagrammatic relationship between the names "Bilioso" and "Bassiolo," proposed by Fleay, and the parallel which he saw between *Usher*, IV.v.113, and Bilioso's phrase "a gentleman usher call'd me coxcomb" (III.i.82) seem far-fetched, it is true that both plays satirize gentlemen ushers (see Appendix C). Finally, hunting parties are important in both plays. Even if these parallels are redolent of borrowing, however, there is no way of knowing who borrowed from whom, for the date of *The Malcontent* has not been certainly pinpointed between 1600 and 1604.[16]

THE PLAY AND ITS SOURCES

A rivalry between a father and a son is a familiar enough motif, from Plautus' *Casina* to such Renaissance comedies as *The Wisdom of Doctor Dodypoll*, Marston's *The Fawn*, and Fletcher's *Monsieur Thomas*, and sometimes the motif includes a secret marriage by the son. Koeppel thought *Doctor Dodypoll* to be a source for Chapman's *Gentleman Usher*,[17] but the two are not very similar and in fact no

[16] M. L. Wine, ed., *The Malcontent*, Regents Renaissance Drama Series (Lincoln, 1964), pp. xiv–xvi.

[17] Emil Koeppel, *Quellen-Studien zu den Dramen George Chapman's, Philip Massinger's und John Ford's*, Quellen und Forschungen, Heft 82 (Strassburg, 1897), 221. F. L. Schoell thought Chapman to be the author of *Dodypoll* (see Parrott, *The Comedies*, p. 754 n.). In both plays the father-rival is a duke named Alphonso.

direct source of the main plot has been found. Chapman may have put together elements gleaned from various sources. Corteza's reference to Adelasia, incorrectly associating her with a self-inflicted disfigurement, raises the possibility that the Adelasia story in William Painter's *Palace of Pleasure* may have suggested the clandestine marriage of Vincentio and Margaret, for the Adelasia story involves such a marriage, but the possibility is perhaps not very strong. Parrott traced the disfigurement motif to the Parthenia story in Sidney's *Arcadia*, Book I, which Chapman must have known and which was also the source for the anonymous play *The Trial of Chivalry*; and to the tale of Florinda told by Painter, Novel 53, and earlier in the tenth novella of the *Heptameron* of Margaret of Navarre. The identity of names of Chapman's heroine and of the author of the *Heptameron* is suggestive, for, as we shall see, Chapman adopted another author's name for one of the characters in the subplot; and, although Corteza's reference is confused (she names Pettie's *Petite Palace of Pleasure* rather than Painter's *Palace of Pleasure*), the reference nonetheless suggests that Chapman at least knew that there was such a story in Painter and had probably read it. In any case, neither Sidney's nor Painter's version alone provided all the details which Chapman included. The Painter version has a self-inflicted mutilation (with a blow from a stone, motivated by a desire to discourage an unwanted suitor); the Sidney version has a mutilation by a chemical substance (not self-inflicted), a contest in generosity like Vincentio's and Margaret's (V.iv.95–121), and a miraculous cure. Perhaps it was Chapman who first combined elements from the two versions.[18]

The source of the Strozza subplot has also been unknown, but I have recently discovered it in the tenth chapter of a Latin work called *De Abditis Nonnullis ac Mirandis Morborum & Sanationum Causis Liber* (On Some Hidden and Miraculous Causes of Diseases and Cures), by a fifteenth-century Florentine physician and savant, Antonio Benivieni. First published posthumously in 1507, the work, a collection of one hundred eleven purportedly true case-histories, finds a place in medical histories for its treatment of "hidden" (i.e., internal) causes: because some of its accounts contain the earliest known descriptions of systematic autopsies, it has earned for Benivieni the title "father of pathological anatomy." The "miraculous" histories, however, several of them tinged with the Christian Platonism

[18] Parrott, *The Comedies*, p. 755.

of Benivieni's associate Marcilio Ficino, have little medical significance and have remained relatively obscure.[19] But Chapman used one of these, borrowing every major event and several key phrases from the case-history of a young Florentine named Gaspar; he also borrowed the name of Strozza's doctor (with its appropriate etymological sense, "welcome") from the Latin form of Benivieni's name, Benevenius. Both Benivieni's Gaspar and Chapman's Strozza suffer arrow wounds "near the midriff," each has the arrowhead fixed in "the bottom of his solid rib" (such at least was Chapman's interpretation of *in intima costa*), and each can be treated only by having the rib broken and the wound made larger. Both patients reject the only available treatment, preferring death by suicide; Gaspar thinks of three possible means (hanging, leaping into the Arno River, or leaping into a well), and Strozza echoes two of these: leaping into the sea rather than the Arno (Chapman's setting is Italian, but unlocalized) and leaping from a turret rather than into a well.[20] Both Gaspar and Strozza are restrained from suicide by people who preach to them continually to put themselves into God's hands, and both experience a miraculous transport during which both predict the arrival of friends and foretell the day on which their arrowheads will fall out. Finally, both make a trip to Rome, though (so far as we know) only Strozza's trip is a pilgrimage and only Gaspar dies there.

There are differences between the two accounts. Gaspar lost his gift of prophecy as soon as the arrowhead fell from his side, whereas

[19] Jean Jacquot found the work and noticed the resemblance between the names of its author and Strozza's doctor, but he did not mention Chapter X, which Chapman used; he read another chapter (XXVI) involving an imbedded arrow and rightly concluded that it had little resemblance to the Strozza plot (*George Chapman [1559–1634]: Sa Vie, Sa Poésie, Son Théâtre, Sa Pensée* [Paris, 1951], p. 94 n.). In Appendix A, I present the Latin text of Chapter X, together with my translation. For Benivieni's life see the *Dizionario Biografico degli Italiani*, VIII (Rome, 1966), 543–545. Portions of my analysis have appeared previously in "The Genesis of the Strozza Subplot in George Chapman's *The Gentleman Usher*," *Publications of the Modern Language Association*, LXXXIII (1968), 1448–1453.

[20] Chapman could simply have mistranslated, but there is an interesting parallel between his version and Marston's *Antonio's Revenge*, IV.i.206–208: "Distraught and raving, from a turret's top/ He threw his body in the high-swoll'n sea;/ And . . . he headlong topsy-turvy ding'd down. . . ." For other parallels with that play see above, n. 10. See also *Gentleman Usher*, V.iii.6.

Strozza is still using some sort of superior power to cross-examine Medice at the end of the play. Alerted by the development in the source, we can find some indication of a weakening of Strozza's power following his cure. He anticipates the ending of his "powers" (V.ii.41), but he could mean merely that he will die someday. More strikingly, he knows that Vincentio is in danger, but he seems to have forgotten it until Benevenius happens to mention the prince's name (V.ii.50), and then he does not know where or how Vincentio has been imperiled; by contrast, he had earlier predicted the very day of his own cure, and he had known not only that Vincentio was coming to see him but that Pogio had just parted from the prince (IV.iii.100). And his awareness of Medice's baseness at the end is, after all, not materially different from his "conceit" long before his injury that Medice was a "fustian lord" (I.i.107). If this apparent weakening was intentionally included by Chapman, it was probably suggested by Gaspar's total loss of the prophetic gift in the source, and it may mean that even a divine gift becomes corrupted and weakened once the mystical contact with its divine origin (through the symbolic arrowhead) has been broken. But in any case Strozza is clearly a better man for his experience: the wisdom and the "judicial patience" that he has gained are not transitory. And the arrowhead itself remains as a tangible symbol of divinely inspired wisdom, to be placed in St. Peter's and "visibly . . . stir the soul" of any other struggling pilgrim to "gratitude and progress in the use/ Of my tried patience" (V.ii.38–41).

A more obvious change is in the names. Chapman changed the name of his protagonist from Gaspar to Strozza, and it is interesting to find a character (a villain, to be sure) in Marston's *Antonio's Revenge*, Gaspar Strotzo, who holds both these names. The name "Strozza" might have been suggested, alternatively, by another case history in Benivieni's work (chapter fifty-four), that of one Philippus Stroza, perhaps to be identified as Filippo Strozzi the elder (d. 1491). Finally, it might have been suggested by the name of the more famous Filippo Strozzi the younger (d. 1538), powerful enemy of the Florentine Medicis; Piero de' Medici is casually mentioned in the chapter of Benivieni's work which Chapman was following, and the villain in Chapman's play is named Medice. His name is twice spelled *Medici* in the quarto, and he calls Strozza his "despiteful enemy" (III.i.7). Whatever its source, the name "Strozza" is used for its semantic significance: it is the Italian word for throat. In

Marston's play, the name "Strotzo" becomes meaningful when the villain is strangled; in Chapman's, the name "Strozza" is meaningful for its association with the name "Cynanche", a Greek word which usually means a throat disease but which is made from two roots meaning dog-collar. There is perhaps an ambiguity here, for a wife who is a sore throat to her husband is scarcely an ideal wife; perhaps Strozza would think her a sore throat in Act I, when she nags him about hunting for boar—a scene, by the way, which may echo Venus' appeal in Shakespeare's *Venus and Adonis*, ll. 613–714. But after he is wounded, Cynanche's nagging is the instrument which dissuades him from suicide and helps him to assume "judicial patience"; as a result, he achieves his "inspired rapture" and utters several paeans of gratitude for his wife's wisdom. It is also at her instigation that Strozza vows to place the arrowhead in St. Peter's in Rome. In thus restraining and guiding her husband, Strozza's collar, his "good angel," performs the function that a collar traditionally performed in the emblematic literature of the Renaissance: it disciplined its wearer.[21] Clearly, the choice of these two names was deliberate.

The introduction of a wife is itself an innovation by Chapman, for in Benivieni's story the spiritual counselor of Gaspar is a friend, Marioctus. A wife is patently more useful to Chapman's conception than is a friend, for she makes possible a fairly elaborate parallel between the established legal marriage of Strozza and Cynanche and the rebellious, self-performed marriage of Vincentio and Margaret. Both marriages are "far remov'd from Custom's popular sects" (IV.ii.199), and both are marked by a mysterious unity of husband and wife. According to Strozza, an ideal wife like Cynanche becomes one with her husband,

> Feeling his joys and griefs with equal sense;
> And, like the twins Hippocrates reports,
> If he fetch sighs, she draws her breath as short;
> If he lament, she melts herself in tears;
> If he be glad, she triumphs; if he stir,
> She moves his way, in all things his sweet ape,

---

[21] The most famous example of this symbolism is George Herbert's later poem "The Collar," concerning which F. E. Hutchinson wrote that the "collar was in common use to express discipline" (*The Works of George Herbert* [Oxford, 1953], p. 531).

> And is in alterations passing strange,
> Himself divinely varied without change.   (IV.iii.16–23)

Margaret vows to be such a wife to Vincentio:

> In and for you shall be my joys and woes:
> If you be sick, I will be sick though well;
> If you be well, I will be well though sick;
> Yourself alone my complete world shall be
> Even from this hour to all eternity.   (IV.ii.176–180)

The Platonic basis of Strozza's marriage is evident from his imagery in speaking of Cynanche's "wing'd spirit" and her "beauty, ravishing and pure" (IV.iii.5–7) to his recognition that she subordinates her physical comforts to "more worthy objects," the rare pleasures of enjoying her husband's "virtuous gifts" (V.ii.24 ff.). Similar to this is Vincentio's reaffirmation of his desire for Margaret despite her loss of beauty:

> . . . do not wrong me so
> To think my love the shadow of your beauty.
> I woo your virtues, which as I am sure
> No accident can alter or impair,
> So be you certain nought can change my love.
>
> (V.iv.95–99)

Strozza's implicit sun image for Margaret's beauty (V.iv.134) is ultimately Platonic. The structure of Act IV reinforces the Platonic parallel between these two couples: Vincentio and Margaret perform their clandestine rites in IV.ii, between the two scenes in which Cynanche's ideal housewifery is fully revealed.

In the last two scenes of Act IV the contrasting standards of Alphonso and his helpers are fully shown; in particular, Lasso offers his daughter not a Platonic union but a marriage to which "time and judgment will conform" her mind (IV.v.27). The play is partly built upon such contrasts between the married couples and an establishment comprised of people foolish, villainous, or misguided. The conspiracy of the establishment is disorganized and multifarious, from the amorous "iniquity" of Alphonso with its silly masque and its proud despotism to the mindless sensuality of Corteza which descends to willful treachery; and to the ignorant and petty malignity of Medice with its murderous plot against Strozza. The counter-conspiracy of the innocents, though diverse, is unified in philosophy and sentiment. Its unity and its contrast with the conspiracy of mischief against which it must work are highlighted by parallels of situation and utterance, especially involving Strozza and Margaret.[22]

Both Strozza and Margaret are afflicted with unbearable pain, and each has an adviser during his crisis. Strozza threatens to "cast me headlong down" from some turret (IV.i.73), justifying his intention by an assertion of "the Stoic belief in the propriety of suicide," a belief which he shares with the Senecan Hercules.[23] As permeated as some Chapman plays are with Senecan Stoicism— Higgins states that to Chapman, Stoicism was a "necessary element in the character of the 'complete man'"[24]—in this case Strozza's adviser, the saintly Cynanche, explicitly denies the propriety of Herculean "valor" (IV.i.55–56) and urges instead the Christianized Stoicism of patience. She succeeds in her urging, and under her guidance he moves even beyond Christian Stoicism to experience a Neo-Platonic ecstasy in which he becomes "nought else but soul."[25] Margaret too, in mental agony because she thinks Vincentio is dead, would "cast myself down headlong from this tower" (V.iii.6), though her motive is not Stoic. She is advised not by a saintly spouse but by the treacherous Corteza, who, far from dissuading her, goads her on with the examples of suffering heroines from romantic literature (V.iii.10, 23, 32). When, afraid to die, Margaret decides to destroy her beauty, her stated motives are little more than expressions of guilt and anger: she would dissuade the advances of men (V.iii.48), attone for Vincentio's death (V.iii.75), and shame Alphonso (V.iii. 81–82). Later, however, we can see a philosophic resemblance between her act and Strozza's ecstasy. In what Hardin Craig called

22 In III.ii, Chapman brings together all the important characters and in 286 ff. stages the conspiracies of the play *en tableau*. After Corteza has epitomized the folly of the courtly establishment with her drunk scene, the parties separate to people the stage in whispering groups: Alphonso and Lasso planning a forced marriage, Vincentio and Strozza counter-planning, and Medice and a huntsman planning murder.

23 Michael Higgins, "The Development of the 'Senecal Man': Chapman's *Bussy D'Ambois* and Some Precursors," *Review of English Studies*, XXIII (1947), 29.

24 *Ibid.*, p. 32. Cf. J. W. Wieler, *George Chapman—The Effect of Stoicism upon His Tragedies* (New York, 1949).

25 For an analysis of the Neo-Platonism of the incident, see Jacquot, pp. 94–96.

a surprisingly "literal concomitancy of physical and psychic states,"[26] Strozza has become "nought else but soul," casting off his flesh even while still alive (V.ii.13). As Margaret tells Vincentio, however, she has despaired of fulfilling their love in a Platonic ecstasy while they live and awaits death, when their love "must needs be *all* in soul" and beauty will be of "no respect with love's eternity" (V.iv. 112–115). Destroying her beauty, then, has been her way of casting off her flesh while still retaining it in mere life, for beauty is the inspiration—the "ushering fire," Vincentio has called it (IV.ii.156) —of love.[27]

Significantly, it is Benevenius who cures Margaret's deformity. He has been powerless to cure Strozza; but, presumably taught by Strozza to "build his cares hereafter upon heaven/ More than on earthly med'cines" (IV.iii.72–73), he now calls upon heaven, art, nature, and Medea's "elixir" to restore Margaret's beauty. Thus we have still another link between Margaret and Strozza. Benevenius has also begun Vincentio's cure and will himself conjoin the hands of the lovers in fleshly recognition of the Platonic union of their "constant hearts" (V.iv.139–140). The curing of Margaret's physical deformity by the hands of the physician whom Strozza has schooled symbolizes his correction of her misapprehension concerning the attainability of Platonic union in this world. In much the same way has Strozza been cured of his wound and his despair by Cynanche.

Margaret, of course, has not always held this sin of despair; she has been driven to it by a political climate in which the duke can, in effect, prefer whom he pleases, marry whom he pleases, kill whom he pleases. Before that it was Margaret who proposed to Vincentio that they "ratify [their] hearts' true vows/ Which no external violence shall dissolve" (IV.ii.145–146). In taking that stance she was once again contrasting the corrupt courtly circle with the Platonically pure couples, and once again there is a striking parallel with Strozza to reinforce the contrast. Here the parallel is political. Margaret has prefaced her proposal to Vincentio with the following apology for men of strength:

> Are not the laws of God and Nature more
> Than formal laws of men?.   .   .   .
>
>   .   .   .   .

26 "Ethics in the Jacobean Drama: The Case of Chapman," *Essays in Dramatic Literature: The Parrott Presentation Volume* (Princeton, 1935), p. 38.
27 Harbage, p. 241.

> Or shall laws made to curb the common world,
> That would not be contain'd in form without them,
> Hurt them that are a law unto themselves?
>
> (IV.ii.133–139)

The sentiment is identical to Strozza's when he accuses Alphonso of abusing his power:

> And what's a prince? Had all been virtuous men,
> There never had been prince upon the earth
> And so no subject: all men had been princes.
> A virtuous man is subject to no prince
> But to his soul and honor, which are laws
> That carry fire and sword within themselves,
> Never corrupted, never out of rule. (V.iv.56–62)

The notion is familiar enough from certain other passages in Chapman, notably *Bussy D'Ambois*, II.i.194–204; in *The Gentleman Usher* it codifies the contrast between people like Alphonso and Lasso and people like Strozza and Margaret.

The doctrine of "virtuous men" is illuminated by the theme of degree as it recurs cyclically throughout the play. There is considerable concern, both serious and comic, with rank: Margaret assures her father that she would not marry beneath her station (IV.v.7); both Margaret and Lasso are shocked that Bassiolo calls Vincentio Vince (IV.ii.109, V.iv.170); Pogio justifies his petty instability before the menial Fungus by claiming "Gentility must be fantastical" (II.i.139); Corteza perverts tradition by assuring Medice that "It becomes noblemen to do nothing well" (I.ii.136); and Medice is finally exposed as having done a "mighty scandal" to "honor" (nobility) by assuming noble rank to which he has no claim save the voice of "an old sorceress" (V.iv.261). But the degree which really matters in this play is of a different sort: that of Strozza, for instance, whose voice comes not from a gypsy sorceress but from a heavenly source and—to put the contrast in another way—who sees from "the stars . . . as in a sort of crystal globes" (IV.iii.61–62), not with Corteza's "blue crystal full of sorcery," her "old wife's eye" (IV.iv.54–55). Vincentio explicitly states the principles:

> . . . some
> Have extraordinary spirits . . .
> And will not stand in their society

On birth and riches, but on worth and virtue.

. . . Be he poor
Or basely born, so he be rich in soul
And noble in degrees of qualities,
He shall be my friend sooner than a king.   (III.ii.57–65)

This is not the degree familiar from Ulysses' speech in Shakespeare's
Troilus and Cressida (I.iii.85–137) or from Menenius' fable of the belly
in *Coriolanus* (I.i.99–167) or from Hooker's *Laws of Ecclesiastical
Polity*—all statements of the orthodox Renaissance social and political
system based on class and position. Instead of that system, which in
this play sanctions the tyranny of a father over his children and a
duke over his subjects, Vincentio offers a system based on strength
of character, on "virtue" as Chapman usually uses the word. Vincentio's statement is disingenuous, for it is designed to dupe Bassiolo,
but his sentiment is taken seriously in the play. The greatest "scandal"
which Medice has committed is assuming nobility to which he has
no claim *in merit*: he has been "rais'd to honor's height/ Without
the help of virtue or of art/ Or, to say true, of any honest part"
(I.i.110–112); he is incapable of treating with due respect either
his servants or his supposed peers (except possibly Corteza, who
alone says anything good of him); and the scandal which he has
done his own class (the gypsies) is as great as that which he has done
to the court of Alphonso. In fact, Alphonso's violations of the play's
concept of degree are probably the greatest in the play. That he has
unnaturally abused his parental authority is evident from the image
which both Strozza and Margaret independently use of him: he is
like Cronos, who swallowed his own children at birth (V.iii.82,
V.iv.54–55). Strozza's identification of him with Nero (V.iv.42) and
the implication that he is greater than common men only in his
faults (V.iv.65) condemn his political leadership. And the terms in
which Alphonso's love for Margaret is presented imply disruption
of the natural order: Pogio's "Will his antiquity never leave his
iniquity?" (I.i.31); Vincentio's complaint that he does not know
"whether yet/ I shall enjoy a stepdame or a wife" (I.i.83–84); even
Corteza's emphasis on Alphonso's age however vigorous (I.ii.38,
III.ii.233), though she of course supports the duke's cause. Bassiolo
sums it up: "Who saw ever summer mix'd with winter?/ There
must be equal years where firm love is" (III.ii.150–151). The possible

bawdy pun in *firm love* and his self-serving continuation in the following lines do not detract from the centric idea. Alphonso's defects in political and personal degree work the greater mischief because they work toward the separation of two lovers who are capable of a mysterious Platonic unity.

Thus are heroic and romantic materials, taken from at least two or three different sources, thematically and dramatically unified. With some exceptions, the characters around whom these materials are constructed are drawn with little subtlety. Some of them are little more than types familiar from Italian comedy: Alphonso is the old man who lusts for a young bride and behaves like a young lover, Lasso the interfering old father of a rebellious daughter, Medice the upstart courtier and almost motiveless villain. Even Vincentio is simply drawn. He is shrewdly aware of the progression of Bassiolo's state of mind and at times audaciously funny in gulling him; he is courageously steadfast to Margaret through two different crises; but he is essentially the type of the son whose clever intrigues succeed in overcoming parental opposition. Interesting ethical questions can be raised concerning his perversion of Renaissance concepts of friendship in the gulling of Bassiolo, but they do little to complicate his character. Cynanche too is a type: although the ambiguity in her name, discussed earlier, suggests that critics may have over-simplified the idealism of her treatment, she is basically her husband's helpmate in sickness and in health; her picture is highlighted, however, by one or two interesting details such as her aversion to grand social affairs, an aversion which she sets aside at her husband's special request (I.i.72–77). Strozza appears more complex, and he has sometimes been taken to be Chapman's own spokesman; Parrott called him "one of the most remarkable [characters] in Chapman's comedies," and Una Ellis-Fermor thought him worthy of comparison with "the most notable Jacobean figures."[28] But in the end one has trouble saying much more than that he is a faithful friend who almost magically has his Stoicism qualified by Christian Neo-Platonism which conditions all his behavior. Of all the characters in the romantic plot, Margaret is probably the best developed: one notices her plucky spirit in effectively rejecting Alphonso's overtures in the opening acts, in finding a means to encourage Vincentio (the modest but obvious "y'are welcome," I.ii.151), and in first suggesting

[28] Parrott, *The Comedies*, p. 760; Ellis-Fermor, *The Jacobean Drama: An Interpretation*, 3rd edn. (London, 1953), p. 57.

a clandestine marriage; her playful wit in gulling Bassiolo in a way that will ensure his continued assistance, and yet her occasional pity for her victim; her warmth of emotions for Vincentio when she exchanges vows with him and when, in the last scene, she attempts to free him from those vows; and her combination of anger and despair, of determination and fear when all seems lost in the scene of her defacement (V.iii).

As we shall see, Bassiolo is interestingly drawn as well, but the emphasis in *The Gentleman Usher* is generally upon intrigue and incident, and upon conflicts of philosophic attitudes, more than upon character. The romantic plot holds up well because the intrigues are well plotted, because the characters are made just sufficient to the philosophic burdens they must carry, because the play is philosophically unified, and because it is written in effectively versatile poetry which can be lyrically sweet for the marriage scene or ruggedly conversational in less emotional scenes.

The Gentleman Usher is unusual among Chapman's comedies for the dominance of its romantic plot. His comedies, like most Renaissance comedies, have a romantic core, of course, and in *All Fools* and *Monsieur D'Olive* the romantic element is quite important. But the larger portions of both those plays are given over to comic satire and, in *All Fools*, which is based on Terence's *Heautontimoroumenos*, to Terentian intrigue. In other Chapman comedies, the romantic elements are even more fully submerged beneath realism, satire, even cynicism, and most of them are marked by the modern techniques of the comedy of humors—a genre which Chapman may have given its first big impetus with his early play *An Humorous Day's Mirth*.

Yet there are in *The Gentleman Usher*, as in most contemporary children's plays, conspicuous elements of satire and realism as well. Some of these comic materials are perhaps drawn from current publications, but the only element whose source seems to have been found is Pogio's first dream (see Appendix B). Some of the comic characters are types: Sarpego, for instance, the pedant addicted to Latinate words but not knowing the front from the back of his nightcap, is familiar from Italian comedy and from several English comedies; and Fungus, the doltish servant, belongs to a very old tradition. Others are in the satirical vein of the comedy of humors: Corteza has the "humor of the cup" (III.ii.275) and with it a near incapacity to speak without bawdy double meanings; and Pogio's humors are saying things backwards and delivering bad news, even (at V.iv.156) when there is no bad news to deliver. These two humor characters are effectively amusing, and both are made a part of the main action: Corteza's amorous nature, piqued into matronly jealousy of the young girls who "engross up all the love/ From us poor beldames" (IV.iv.29–30), makes her eager to look for the evidence against Margaret and villainously to abet her disfigurement; and, though less substantially integrated with the main action, Pogio's "unhappy tongue" (I.i.156) serves the dramatic purpose of interrupting the most triumphant moments of both Vincentio (IV.ii. 208) and Strozza (V.ii.64) with disastrous news. Sarpego and Fungus are less effective and have almost nothing to do with the main action; in fact, they both disappear after the second act.

The titular figure, Bassiolo, as the servant who schemes with a son to thwart his father, "is akin to the Roman *servus* and the Italian *cameriere*";[29] it may not be merely coincidental that, early in the play, Sarpego quotes several lines from the titular role of *Curculio*, a Plautine play named for such a scheming slave. But Bassiolo is more schemed against than scheming and is, in that respect, different not only from the Roman slave but from what F. S. Boas called "the most distinctive figure" in some other Chapman comedies, the "character who holds in his hands all the threads of the action."[30] Chapman has alloyed the traditional type with comedy of humors: Bassiolo's humor is described by Strozza as "servile avarice/ And overweening thought of his own worth,/ Ready to snatch at every shade of glory" (I.ii. 170–172). Accordingly, although we do not actively dislike Bassiolo, we do not sympathize with him as we usually do with the Roman slave. Although J. V. Curry has been at some pains to find redeeming traits in Bassiolo,[31] and although Margaret occasionally expresses pity for him, the gentleman usher is from beginning to end a dupe repeatedly described as what he is, a vain fool. At the end, the "discreet usher" is praised by Alphonso because "he saw the fitness of the match/ With freer and more noble eyes than we" (V.iv.150, 176–177); it is true that he has recognized that there "must be equal years where firm love is" (III.ii.151), but the audience knows that Bassiolo is being praised for discretion not his own. Even the witless

[29] Marvin T. Herrick, *Tragicomedy: Its Origin and Development in Italy, France, and England*, Illinois Studies in Language and Literature, XXXIX (Urbana, 1955), 239.

[30] *An Introduction to Stuart Drama* (Oxford, 1946), p. 19.

[31] *Deception in Elizabethan Comedy* (Chicago, 1955), p. 96.

Pogio recalls, impoliticly, "Why, I saw that as well as he, my lord" (V.iv.178), and we know that Bassiolo's motive in furthering Vincentio's cause was vanity. His victimization by Vincentio and again by Margaret could be explained as mere naïvete, perhaps, if the methods which succeed were less outrageous: e.g., he fails to recognize the gulling tactics which Vincentio expressly describes (III.ii.76), and he is clearly flattered by suggestions that he might have been Margaret's lover and that he might be made a nobleman. Unlike Pogio, who knows himself as "the veriest fool on you all" (III.ii. 221), Bassiolo has no awareness of his own limitations: "faith's his fault," says Vincentio (V.i.37), excessive faith in himself. His supervision of the laying of rushes, his directions to the players in the masque, his amorous instructions to Vincentio, his love letter for Margaret, all are of a piece: heavy-handed, officious, and ridiculous. It is a comic irony that this vain incompetent can apparently look forward, at the end of the play, to being made "the duke's minion" (V.iv.159–160), for he clearly wants the "degrees of qualities" requisite to such improvement, according to one important theme in the play: Alphonso has not become a philosopher-king.

In fashioning Bassiolo in this way, Chapman may have been parodying Shakespeare's Malvolio, who is also gulled for his vanity; he may have been satirizing some individual or the institutions of court.[32] Whatever his intentions, he certainly created an effective comic character, and in this case one who is perfectly fused into the main action. As Parrott wrote, "One cannot disentangle the gulling of Bassiolo from the romantic courtship of Vincentio and Margaret,"[33] and similarly one cannot disentangle the gulling from its causes in Bassiolo's nature. Moreover, he links the comic materials of the first two acts with what follows, for he serves in both parts: as officious but incompetent manipulator of his underlings in the opening acts and as manipulated in the later part. He is also involved in several of the main themes. As a gentleman usher, he typifies the courtly establishment against which Vincentio and Margaret must rebel. The household statute books are sometimes quite explicit about a gentleman usher's ceremonial behavior, in particular about his hat; and Chapman seems deliberately to have focused attention

[32] Gentlemen ushers were also satirized in other works at about this time; for a discussion of gentlemen ushers in fact and fiction see Appendix C.

[33] *The Comedies*, p. 759.

on Bassiolo's hat, which functions in somewhat the same way as Osric's hat does for a brief time in Shakespeare's *Hamlet* (V.ii.96–108), as a symbol of courtly facade lacking in inner worth. At his first entrance, leading a noble procession, Bassiolo is bareheaded (I.ii.0.1), but he is certainly carrying his hat; he is noted for the "constant fashion of his hat" (I.ii.164); Vincentio is advised to corrupt him with gifts of hats (I.ii.174); his removal of his hat at II.i.90 is an occasion for Vincentio's subtle ridicule; and in the crucial scene of discovery he can swear to his truthfulness by nothing more sacred than his hat held over his heart (V.i.132). With the courtly ceremony which Bassiolo's hat epitomizes, Vincentio's diction at one point explicitly contrasts his own Platonic relationship with Margaret: he swears constancy by "love's *ushering* fire,/ Fore-melting beauty" (IV.ii.156–157). The impact of this contrast is fully realized a little later when, immediately after the ethereal vows of Vincentio and Margaret and just before the tender kiss which symbolically consummates their marriage, Bassiolo enters with a pun, witting or unwitting, which debases the Platonic vows of the couple. Finally, Bassiolo also illustrates a facet of the theme of degree: as a mere gentleman, he is led to treat Vincentio as an equal; by Vincentio's expressed standards of "degrees of qualities," this would be satisfactory if Bassiolo had the "qualities," but as we have seen he does not.

It was surely because of his position linking actions, tones, and themes that Chapman named the play for Bassiolo; and it was presumably his complete integration with the main action which made Una Ellis-Fermor conclude that this play came as close as any to duplicating the "exquisite Terentian balance of mischievous intrigue with poignant or pathetic romance." [34] Because of its successful fusion of "comical satire" into a romantic plot which approaches disaster, has tragic passions, stresses incident over characterization, and is built around a series of sensations and surprises, Parrott and others have called *The Gentleman Usher* an early example of tragicomedy. Marvin Herrick found it lacking the complexity of plot which marks the "fully developed tragicomedies" of Beaumont and Fletcher. [35] Others have argued that the comedy and the romance are not in fact fused: Eugene Waith felt that Chapman "combines the satire and the romance mechanically, keeping each separate

[34] Ellis-Fermor, p. 56 *n*.
[35] Herrick, p. 241.

from the other";[36] and Muriel Bradbrook that the "different moods, though technically well linked, do not cohere."[37] Although their criticisms include the Bassiolo portion of the comedy, most complaints of disunity are directed against the first two acts. Even Parrott spoke of the "futilities" of those acts, and others have used stronger terms. The criticism may be slightly exaggerated, for much of the matter of the first two acts is somehow relevant to the play, though at times the relevance is superficial. The opening acts expose all the characters and their relative positions in the prospective conflicts. The second-act masque, apparently a full-scale masque with a variety of dances and the anti-masque of the bugs, dominates the opening section in its preparation and its performance, and it does not appeal to modern tastes; of course, we do not have the songs and dances and costumes upon which it chiefly depended, but the satirical bombast of Sarpego and the distorted logic of Pogio and Fungus make for lean humor. At its best, the masque distracts from the progress of the play, but its bare relevance must be admitted: its evident theme, the wooing of coy maidens by scorned suitors, is designed to assist Alphonso in his quest for Margaret even as it in fact parodies that quest. Its rustic setting, moreover, as well as its theme, associates it with the first-act show in which Alphonso is figured as returning wounded from a rustic chase. Like the masque, this show parodies Alphonso's suit, especially in Strozza's speech, pasted together from various romantic elements. The ritual releasing of Alphonso's bonds by Margaret is among the elements which link up with particular parts of the later action: it contrasts with the binding of Margaret and Vincentio in IV.ii. Similarly, the pretended wounding of Alphonso anticipates the wounding of Strozza in the more serious part of the play,[38] as indeed the mock hunt of the first act anticipates the real hunt of Act III and the hunt for Vincentio and Margaret which Corteza announces (IV.iv.52–53). Henry M. Weidner found a more pervasive relationship between the opening acts and the later part: in his view, the play-acting of the first two acts amounts to a collection of superficial ceremonies lacking true substance and thus demonstrating the defects of the courtly party

[36] *The Pattern of Tragicomedy in Beaumont and Fletcher*, Yale Studies in English, CXX (New Haven, 1952), 80.

[37] *The Growth and Structure of Elizabethan Comedy* (London, 1955), p. 173.

[38] *Ibid.*, p. 237 n. Miss Bradbrook adds that "it does not really relate with the subsequent scene."

who plan the ceremonies; contrasted with these are the true ceremonies of the later part, lacking conventional form but containing
"true decorum"—Strozza's ecstatic state, Margaret's marriage, and
later her cure.[39] Right to the end this contrast prevails: Alphonso's
plan to celebrate Vincentio's marriage "in greater majesty/ Than
ever grac'd our greatest ancestry" (V.iv.294–295), though a satis-
fying recognition of the young couple's Platonic union, is a futile
confirmation of the formless ceremony of IV.ii. There are links, then,
among the various parts of the play, and at the very least it is an
important experiment in a genre which would soon dominate
English comedy for a time.

Apart from the opening acts, which do deserve censure if only
because they are too long, criticism of *The Gentleman Usher* has been
generally favorable, but there are sharply divided opinions. The
earliest known commentator on the play, Gerard Langbaine, thought
it only "indifferent," though he had "heard it commended by some,
for a good Comedy."[40] Critics as diverse as Lowell, Swinburne, and
Ellis-Fermor have liked it, especially for the poetry of its romantic
scenes.[41] A. W. Ward thought it simply a bad play, but he conceded
that the marriage scene was "finely-written."[42] Most modern opinion
tends to call it one of Chapman's best comedies, equal to or just
below *All Fools*.[43]

---

[39] "The Dramatic Uses of Homeric Idealism: The Significance of Theme
and Design in George Chapman's *The Gentleman Usher*," *Journal of English
Literary History*, XXVIII (1961), 121–136.

[40] *An Account of the English Dramatick Poets* (Oxford, 1691), p. 63. Else-
where he called *The Gentleman Usher* "A Play which deserves no great
Commendation, and I question whether ever 'twas Acted" (*The Lives and
Characters of the English Dramatick Poets* [London, (1699)], p. 18).

[41] James Russell Lowell, *The Old English Dramatists* (London, 1892),
pp. 86–87; Algernon Swinburne, *George Chapman: A Critical Essay* (London,
1875), pp. 61–62; Ellis-Fermor, p. 58.

[42] *A History of English Dramatic Literature to the Death of Queen Anne*, II
(London, 1899), 435–437.

[43] The two most recent full-length studies of Chapman disagree with
each other about the merits of this play: Charlotte Spivack called it
"not only a highly successful example of tragicomedy but, from the view-
point of dramatic structure and coherence, one of the best plays that
Chapman ever wrote" (*George Chapman* [New York, 1967], p. 85); Millar
MacLure wrote that it "is on the face of it an absurd play, a real gallimaufry,
weak in construction and faltering in illusion" (*George Chapman: A Critical
Study* [Toronto, 1966], p. 95).

This edition has been helped by suggestions from Samuel Schoenbaum, Melvin H. Wolf, Bertrand A. Goldgar, and Cyrus Hoy. Robert Ornstein kindly made available to me a draft of the preface to his forthcoming old-spelling edition of *The Gentleman Usher*. Akihiro Yamada graciously gave permission for citations from his unpublished edition of the play, which I partially collated. I owe a large debt to the British Museum and to the other libraries whose copies of the play I have used. Finally, I must express my gratitude to the John Simon Guggenheim Memorial Foundation for making possible a leave of absence during which I completed a portion of the work on this edition.

JOHN HAZEL SMITH

Brandeis University

THE GENTLEMAN USHER

[DRAMATIS PERSONAE

ALPHONSO, *the duke*
PRINCE VINCENTIO, *son of Alphonso*
MEDICE (*formerly* MENDICE), *a pretended nobleman and favorite of Alphonso*
STROZZA, *a nobleman and friend of Vincentio*   5
LASSO, *an earl*
BASSIOLO, *gentleman usher to Lasso*
POGIO, *nephew of Strozza*
BENEVENIUS, *a doctor*
JULIO, *a guard*   10
SARPEGO, *a pedant*
FUNGUS, *a servant of Lasso*
A SERVANT *of Medice*

MARGARET, *daughter of Lasso*
CORTEZA, *sister of Lasso*   15
CYNANCHE, *wife of Strozza*
A MAID (*ancilla*)

---

3. *Medice*] see Introduction, p. xix.

3. *Mendice*] probably suggested by two Italian words: *mendico*, a beggar, and *mendace*, "false, lying ... a counterfeite" (Florio). See Introduction, p. xvi.

5. *Strozza*] "the winde pipe or gullet, or ... throat" (Florio). See Introduction, pp. xix–xx.

6. *Lasso*] "... wearie, tyred, faint, or weake. Also an interjection of lamentation alas" (Florio).

7. *Bassiolo*] perhaps related to *basso*, low, or *basoso*, stupid, or conceivably *basciolo*, "a liuely kisse, a busse, full of kisses" (Florio). See p. 136, *n*. 15.

8. *Pogio*] perhaps from *poggio*, Italian word for hill but here perhaps suggesting a blockhead, from the sense "a blocke to get vp on horsebacke" (Florio). But see Appendix B.

9. *Benevenius*] see Introduction, p. xviii.

11. *Sarpego*] perhaps a form of *serpigo*, the name of a skin disease causing itching.

12. *Fungus*] Latin word for mushroom, used figuratively in Plautus for a dolt.

15. *Corteza*] perhaps ironically from *cortezza* (as her name is sometimes spelled in Q), Italian for brevity.

16. *Cynanche*] a Greek word for a throat disease, etymologically meaning a dog-collar. See Introduction, p. xx.

17. *ancilla*] I take this as a Latin common noun rather than a proper name. She plays no role in the only scene in which she appears (V.ii); she is perhaps a nurse, though she could be a remnant of some undeveloped thought of Chapman's; Yamada thought she might be a ghost of revision.

Pages, Attendants, Servants, Maids, Huntsmen, Guard

Figures in the First Entertainment
    Enchanter   20
    Sylvanus, *attempted by Medice*
    Strozza, *who completed Medice's role*
    Alphonso *bound*
    Spirits, *played by pages*

Figures in the Second Entertainment   25
    Sarpego
    Broom-Man, *played by Pogio*
    Rush-Man, *played by Fungus*
    Broom-Maid
    Rush-Maid   30
    Man-Bug
    Woman-Bug
    A Sylvan
    A Nymph]

19–34.] Presumably all these roles were played by boys who had other roles in the play (huntsmen, etc.), but only the assignments identified are clear from the play.

The Gentleman Usher

Enter Strozza, Cynanche, *and* Pogio.

STROZZA.

Haste, nephew. What, a sluggard? Fie, for shame.
Shall he that was our morning cock turn owl
And lock out daylight from his drowsy eyes?

POGIO.

Pray pardon me for once, lord uncle, for I'll be sworn I had
such a dream this morning. Methought one came with a   5
commission to take a sorrel curtal that was stol'n from him,
wheresoever he could find him. And because I feared he
would lay claim to my sorrel curtal in my stable, I ran to the
smith to have him set on his mane again, and his tail presently, that the commission-man might not think him a curtal.   10
And when the smith would not do it, I fell a-beating of him,
so that I could not wake for my life till I was revenged on
him.

CYNANCHE.

This is your old valor, nephew, that will fight sleeping as well
as waking.   15

POGIO.

'Slud, aunt, what if my dream had been true, as it might
have been for anything I knew? There's never a smith in
Italy shall make an ass of me in my sleep if I can choose.

STROZZA.

Well said, my furious nephew. But I see

2.] contrasting *cock* as (1) one who alertly wakens people and (2) "one
who fights with pluck and spirit" (*OED*) with *owl* as (1) a bird of night-
time and (2) "wiseacre, solemn dullard" (*OED*).

6. *commission*] order.

6. *curtal*] "a horse with its tail cut short or docked (and sometimes the
ears cropped)" (*OED*); here also, apparently, with its mane cut short. For
the source of this dream, see Appendix B.

16. *'Slud*] 'Sblood, i.e., by God's blood.

19. *furious*] (1) passionate, (2) foolish.

You quite forget that we must rouse today   20
The sharp-tusk'd boar, and blaze our huntsmanship
Before the duke.

POGIO.

Forget, lord uncle? I hope not. You think belike my wits
are as brittle as a beetle, or as skittish as your barbary mare:
one cannot cry "wehee" but straight she cries "tehee."   25

STROZZA.

Well guess'd, cousin Hysteron Proteron.

POGIO.

But which way will the duke's grace hunt today?

STROZZA.

Toward Count Lasso's house his grace will hunt,
Where he will visit his late honor'd mistress.

POGIO.

Who, Lady Margaret, that dear young dame?   30
Will his antiquity never leave his iniquity?

CYNANCHE.

Why, how now, nephew? Turn'd Parnassus lately?

27. today?] Q corr. (to day); to day.
Q uncorr.

---

20. *rouse*] "cause (game) to rise or issue from cover or lair" (*OED*).
21. *blaze our huntsmanship*] make known our hunting ability.
24. *brittle as a beetle*] Pogio confuses an old proverb, "dull (deaf, dumb, or blind) as a beetle," and makes nonsense of it. By *brittle*, he presumably means unstable (*OED*). A beetle was a heavy implement used to ram paving-stones and was used as "the type of heavy dullness or stupidity" (*OED*). The insect beetle could also have been intended, both as a fragile animal and as the type of intellectual blindness (*OED*).
24. *skittish*] high-strung, like a prized Arabian horse, but Pogio apparently has in mind the sense "fickle, inconstant, changeable" (*OED*).
25. *wehee . . . tehee*] conventional representations, respectively, of a horse's whinny and a human laugh. Pogio confuses the two; hence Strozza's reply.
26. *cousin*] a term for any collateral relative.
26. *Hysteron Proteron*] Greek name for the figure of speech in which "the word or phrase that should properly come last is put first" (*OED*).
28. *Count*] the Continental equivalent of the English title "earl."
29. *late honor'd mistress*] the lady to whom he has paid his respects of late.
31. *antiquity*] old age.
32. *Parnassus*] Greek mountain sacred to Apollo, god of poetry; Cynanche mockingly alludes to Pogio's rhyme of *antiquity–iniquity*. Pogio's answer shows that he has never heard of Parnassus.

POGIO.

    Nassus? I know not. But I would I had all the duke's living
    for her sake; I'd make him a poor duke, i'faith.

STROZZA.

    No doubt of that if thou hadst all his living.   35

POGIO.

    I would not stand dreaming of the matter as I do now.

CYNANCHE.

    Why, how do you dream, nephew?

POGIO.

    Marry, all last night methought I was tying her shoestring.

STROZZA.

    What, all night tying her shoestring?

POGIO.

    Ay, that I was, and yet I tied it not neither; for as I was   40
    tying it, the string broke, methought, and then methought,
    having but one point at my hose, methought, I gave her that
    to tie her shoe withal.

CYNANCHE.

    A point of much kindness, I assure you.

POGIO.

    Whereupon, in the very nick, methought, the count came   45
    rushing in, and I ran rushing out, with my heels about my
    hose for haste.

STROZZA.

    So; will you leave your dreaming and dispatch?

POGIO.

    Mum, not a word more. I'll go before and overtake you
    presently.   *Exit.*   50

CYNANCHE.

    My lord, I fancy not these hunting sports,
    When the bold game you follow turns again

---

33. *Nassus*] cf. Mendoza's ignorance of "Gisthus" (Aegisthus) in Marston's *Malcontent* I.v.9.

33. *living*] income (which Pogio would give up for Margaret).

38. *Marry*] by Mary, a mild oath.

42. *point*] a cord used to attach the hose (breeches) to the doublet.
Cynanche's answer puns on another meaning, "instance."

46–47. *heels . . . hose*] another ignorant reversal of words: with his only
point gone, Pogio's hose (breeches) fell about his heels. Cf. l. 49.

48. *dispatch*] hurry.

And stares you in the face. Let me behold
A cast of falcons on their merry wings,
Daring the stooped prey that shifting flies;   55
Or let me view the fearful hare or hind
Toss'd like a music point with harmony
Of well-mouthed hounds. This is a sport for princes;
The other rude boars yield fit game for boors.

STROZZA.

    Thy timorous spirit blinds thy judgment, wife.   60
Those are most royal sports that most approve
The huntsman's prowess and his hardy mind.

CYNANCHE.

    My lord, I know too well your virtuous spirit.
Take heed, for God's love, if you rouse the boar,
You come not near him, but discharge aloof   65
Your wounding pistol or well-aimed dart.

STROZZA.

    Ay, marry, wife, this counsel rightly flows
Out of thy bosom. Pray thee, take less care;
Let ladies at their tables judge of bores,
Lords in the field. And so farewell, sweet love;   70
Fail not to meet me at Earl Lasso's house.

CYNANCHE.

    Pray pardon me for that: you know I love not
These solemn meetings.

STROZZA.   You must needs for once

---

59. rude boars] *Q corr.* (Boares); rude Boares, *Q uncorr.*; rude; boars *Parrott (Daniel conjecture). The gram-* *matical tidiness achieved by Parrott's pointing is scarcely necessary.*

54–55. *cast . . . Daring . . . stooped prey*] terms from falconry: a *cast* is the number of falcons cast off at a time; *daring* is paralyzing with fear; the *stooped prey* is the prey which is swooped upon. (This passage is the earliest use of the participial adjective *stooped* cited by *OED*.)

57.] Musical imagery: the victim is agitated (*Toss'd*) like the theme of a fugue (*music point*) by the sound (*harmony*) of the baying hounds.

61. *approve*] test.

63. *virtuous*] manly, valiant, possessed of *virtu*.

66. *dart*] arrow or spear.

69. *bores*] with a pun on "boors" (?) and, in the elliptical phrase that follows, "boars."

73. *solemn*] grand, sumptuous.

Constrain your disposition; and indeed
I would acquaint you more with Lady Margaret   75
For special reason.

CYNANCHE.   Very good, my lord;
Then I must needs go fit me for that presence.

STROZZA.
I pray thee do; farewell.   *Exit* Cynanche.
                    Here comes my friend.—

                    Enter Vincentio.

Good day, my lord. Why does your grace confront
So clear a morning with so cloudy looks?   80

VINCENTIO.
Ask'st thou my griefs, that know'st my desp'rate love
Curb'd by my father's stern rivality?
Must not I mourn that know not whether yet
I shall enjoy a stepdame or a wife?

STROZZA.
A wife, prince, never doubt it: your deserts   85
And youthful graces have engag'd so far
The beauteous Margaret that she is your own.

VINCENTIO.
O, but the eye of watchful jealousy
Robs my desires of means t'enjoy her favor.

STROZZA.
Despair not; there are means enow for you: 90
Suborn some servant of some good respect
That's near your choice, who though she needs no wooing
May yet imagine you are to begin
Your strange young love-suit and so speak for you,
Bear your kind letters, and get safe access,   95
All which when he shall do, you need not fear
His trusty secrecy, because he dares not

81. desp'rate] *Q corr.*; desperate *Q uncorr.*
82. rivality?] *Q uncorr.* (riualitie);
riualitie: *Q corr. (this equivalent symbol making room for a correction from* curbd *to* Curbd *in the first word).*

77. *fit*] dress properly.
92. *That's . . . choice*] who has access to your beloved.
92. *who*] refers to *servant.*
93. *are to begin*] have not yet begun.

Reveal escapes whereof himself is author.
Whom you may best attempt, she must reveal;
For if she loves you, she already knows   100
And in an instant can resolve you that.

VINCENTIO.

And so she will, I doubt not. Would to heaven
I had fit time even now to know her mind.
This counsel feeds my heart with much sweet hope.

STROZZA.

Pursue it then; 'twill not be hard t'effect: 105
The duke has none for him but Medice,
That fustian lord who in his buckram face
Bewrays, in my conceit, a map of baseness.

VINCENTIO.

Ay, there's a parcel of unconstrued stuff,
That unknown minion rais'd to honor's height   110
Without the help of virtue or of art
Or, to say true, of any honest part.
O, how he shames my father! He goes like
A prince's footman, in old-fashioned silks
And most times in his hose and doublet only,   115
So miserable that his own few men
Do beg by virtue of his livery;

112. of any] *Shepherd*; nay of *Q* .   shames *Q* .
113. he shames] *Shepherd*; she

---

98. *escapes*] escapades, transgressions.

107. *fustian . . . buckram*] fabrics of poor quality. Fustian was commonly
worn by serving-men; buckram was a coarse linen stiffened with gum or
paste. In either case Medice is by implication a worthless fraud; "men in
buckram" was sometimes proverbial for nonexistent persons (*OED*).

108. *Bewrays . . . map*] reveals, according to my idea, the very image.

109. *unconstrued stuff*] woven fabric not made into anything. *Stuff*, the
fabric, carries on Strozza's cloth image, but there may be a *double entente*:
in contemporary slang, *stuff* may have meant semen (Partridge).

110. *minion*] favorite.

111. *art*] learning.

116. *miserable*] miserly.

117. *livery*] a suit of clothes (commonly in a shade of blue) bearing the
master's coat of arms. The charge is that Medice's servants, poorly paid,
had to "use his livery to beg by, since wearing it they could not be arrested
as masterless men" (Parrott).

> For he gives none, for any service done him
> Or any honor, any least reward.

STROZZA.

> 'Tis pity such should live about a prince;   120
> I would have such a noble counterfeit nail'd
> Upon the pillory and, after, whipp'd
> For his adultery with nobility.

VINCENTIO.

> Faith, I would fain disgrace him by all means
> As enemy to his base-bred ignorance   125
> That, being a great lord, cannot write nor read.

STROZZA.

> For that we'll follow the blind side of him
> And make it sometimes subject of our mirth.

Enter Pogio *post.*

VINCENTIO.

> See, what news with your nephew Pogio?

STROZZA.

> None good, I warrant you.   130

POGIO.

> Where should I find my lord uncle?

STROZZA.

> What's the huge haste with you?

POGIO.

> O, ho, you will hunt today.

STROZZA.

> I hope I will.

POGIO.

> But you may hap to hop without your hope, for the truth is,   135
> Killbuck is run mad.

---

121. *noble counterfeit*] pretended nobleman, possibly with a pun on the coin "noble," worth one-third of a pound.

123. *adultery*] illicit association, perhaps in the sense used by ecclesiastical writers referring to the use of a benefice by someone other than the legal incumbent (*OED*).

127. *follow . . . side*] seek the vulnerable part.

128.1 *post*] hurriedly.

135. *you . . . hope*] according to Yamada, a parody of a proverb, "He that lives in hope dances without music" (Tilley, H 597). *Hop* can mean to dance.

136,138–139. *Killbuck, Ringwood*] names of dogs.

STROZZA.

What's this?

POGIO.

Nay, 'tis true, sir; and Killbuck, being run mad, bit Ringwood so by the left buttock you might have turn'd your nose in it.   140

VINCENTIO.

Out, ass.

POGIO.

By heaven you might, my lord; d'ye think I lie?

VINCENTIO.

'Swounds, might I? —Let's blanket him, my lord. —A blanket here.

POGIO.

Nay, good my Lord Vincentio, by this rush I tell you for 145 good will. —And Venus, your brach there, runs so proud that your huntsman cannot take her down for his life.

STROZZA.

Take her up, fool, thou wouldst say.

POGIO.

Why, sir, he would soon take her down and he could take her up, I warrant her.   150

VINCENTIO.

Well said, hammer, hammer.

---

143. *'Swounds*] by God's wounds.

143. *might I?*] i.e., might I have turn'd my nose in it?

143. *blanket him*] toss him up and down in a blanket.

145. *rush*] Rushes were used for floor-coverings and for torches; in either case, Pogio's oath is ridiculous, since a rush was the type of a worthless object.

146. *brach*] bitch.

146. *runs so proud*] is in such (sexual) heat.

147. *take her down*] Pogio again uses the wrong word. "Take down" was a bawdy idiom referring to the release of sexual excitement through orgasm (Partridge). Strozza corrects to "take up," meaning to bring under control (*OED*).

149. *and*] an, i.e., if.

151. *hammer, hammer*] The first *hammer* may be an imperative meaning keep it up. The second, and probably also the first, is either the hard-headed tool or the yellowhammer (goldfinch), used as a contemptuous epithet.

POGIO.

> Nay, good now, let's alone. —And there's your horse, Gray
> Strozza, too, has the staggers and has struck Bay Beatrice,
> your barbary mare, so, that she goes halting o' this fashion,
> most filthily.   155

STROZZA.

> What poison blisters thy unhappy tongue,
> Evermore braying forth unhappy news?—
> Our hunting sport is at the best, my lord.
> How shall I satisfy the duke, your father,
> Defrauding him of his expected sport?   160
> See, see, he comes.

> *Enter* Alphonso, Medice, Sarpego, *with attendants.*

ALPHONSO.

> Is this the copy of the speech you wrote,
> Signor Sarpego?

SARPEGO.

> It is a blaze of wit poetical;
> Read it, brave duke, with eyes pathetical.   165

ALPHONSO.

> We will peruse it straight. —Well met, Vincentio,
> And good Lord Strozza, we commend you both
> For your attendance. But you must conceive
> 'Tis no true hunting we intend today,
> But an inducement to a certain show   170
> Wherewith we will present our beauteous love,
> And therein we bespeak your company.

VINCENTIO.

> We both are ready to attend your highness.

153. Beatrice] *Shepherd*; Bettrice *Q* .

---

153. *staggers*] a disease of domestic animals characterized by staggering.
153. *struck*] copulated with.
155. *filthily*] disgustingly, if Pogio has used the right word.
158. *at the best*] in excellent condition (ironic).
160.] i.e., of Margaret.
165. *pathetical*] sympathetic.
166. *straight*] directly.
170. *inducement*] prologue.

ALPHONSO.

> See then, here is a poem that requires
> Your worthy censures, offer'd if it like   175
> To furnish our intended amorous show.
> Read it, Vincentio.

VINCENTIO.   Pardon me, my lord;
> Lord Medice's reading will express it better.

MEDICE.

> My patience can digest your scoffs, my lord;
> I care not to proclaim it to the world: 180
> I can nor write nor read, and what of that?
> I can both see and hear as well as you.

ALPHONSO.

> Still are your wits at war.   [*Giving the poem to* Vincentio.]
>   Here, read this poem.

VINCENTIO [*reads*].

> "The red-fac'd sun hath firk'd the floundering shades
> And cast bright 'amel on Aurora's brow—"   185

ALPHONSO.

> High words and strange. Read on, Vincentio.

VINCENTIO [*reads*].

> "The busky groves that gag-tooth'd boars do shroud
> With cringle-crangle horns do ring aloud—"

POGIO.

> My lord, my lord, I have a speech here worth ten of this,
> and yet I'll mend it too.   190

ALPHONSO.

> How likes Vincentio?

VINCENTIO.   It is strangely good;
> No inkhorn ever did bring forth the like.

---

175. *like*] is pleasing.

180. *care . . . proclaim*] do not mind proclaiming.

184. *firk'd . . . shades*] driven away the rolling shadows (of night). *Firk'd* was also slang for copulated (Partridge).

185. *cast . . . brow*] enameled the dawn, a hackneyed image contrasting ridiculously with words like *firk'd*.

186. *High*] exalted in style.

187. *busky*] bushy.

188. *cringle-crangle*] winding in and out.

192. *inkhorn*] container for ink, and a type of pedantry.

Could these brave prancing words with action's spur
Be ridden throughly and managed right,
'Twould fright the audience, and perhaps delight.   195

SARPEGO.

Doubt you of action, sir?

VINCENTIO.   Ay, for such stuff.

SARPEGO.

Then know, my lord, I can both act and teach
To any words. When I in Padua school'd it,
I play'd in one of Plautus' comedies,
Namely *Curculio*, where his part I acted,   200
Projecting from the poor sum of four lines
Forty fair actions.

ALPHONSO.   Let's see that, I pray.

SARPEGO.

Your highness shall command;
But pardon me if, in my actions' heat
Entering in post post haste, I chance to take up   205
Some of your honor'd heels.

POGIO.   Y'ad best leave out
That action for a thing that I know, sir.

SARPEGO.

Then shall you see what I can do without it.

                    [*He brings forth a parasite's costume.*]

ALPHONSO.

See, see, he hath his furniture and all.

SARPEGO.

You must imagine, lords, I bring good news,   210

204. actions'] *this edn.*; actions *Q*;
action's *Shepherd, Parrott.*

---

193. *brave*] showy.
194. *throughly*] thoroughly.
195.] parodying the classic poetic purpose, to instruct and delight.
198. *Padua school'd it*] went to school in Padua, "nursery of arts," in
Shakespeare's words, famous for its university.
200. *his part*] that of Curculio, the parasite.
205. *take up*] trip up.
207. *for . . . sir*] or else.
209. *furniture*] costume.
210. *good news*] Curculio, though unsuccessful in an attempt to borrow
money for his master, is hurrying back with the good news that he has
stolen a valuable ring. In *The Gentleman Usher*, nearly all the news is bad.

Whereof being princely proud, I scour the street
And overtumble every man I meet.   *Exit* Sarpego.

POGIO.

Beshrew my heart if he take up my heels.

Enter Sarpego [*in costume, running about the stage*].

SARPEGO.

Date viam mihi noti, atque ignoti.
Dum ego, hic, officium meum facio.   215
Fugite omnes atque abite, et de via secedite, ne quem
in cursu; aut capite, aut cubito, aut pectore offendam, aut genu.

ALPHONSO.

Thanks, good Signor Sarpego.—
How like you lords this stirring action?

STROZZA.

In a cold morning it were good, my lord,   220
But something harsh upon repletion.

SARPEGO.

Sir, I have ventur'd, being enjoin'd, to eat
Three scholars' commons and yet drew it neat.

POGIO.

Come, sir, you meddle in too many matters; let us, I pray,
tend on our own show at my Lord Lasso's.   225

SARPEGO.

Doing obeisance then to every lord,
I now consort you, sir, even *toto corde*.   *Exit* Sarpego *and* Pogio.

214–217. *Date . . . genu*] *as in* Q,
*because the corruptions could conceivably
have been intended to reflect on the pedant;
the correct reading, from the Teubner edn.
of Plautus by G. Goetz and F. Schoell
(Leipzig, 1893), is as follows: Date*

*uiam mihi, noti atque ignoti, dum ego
hic officium meum/ facio. fugite omnes,
abite et de uia secedite,/ ne quem in
cursu capite aut cubito aut pectore
offendam aut genu. Renaissance edns.
agree.*

214–217.] "Make way for me, friends and strangers, while I do my duty
here. All of you run along, clear out and yield the way so that I don't
hurt anyone in the head, the elbow, the chest, or the knee as I run." The
passage (*Curculio*, ll. 280–282) is only a part of Curculio's speech.

221. *upon repletion*] after eating one's fill.

223. *commons*] meals.

223. *drew it neat*] acted the role well (difficult for a well-filled actor
because Curculio was extremely hungry as he spoke the lines quoted).

227. *consort*] accompany (a recent neologism).

227. *toto corde*] with all my heart.

–16–

MEDICE.

    My lord, away with these scholastic wits;
    Lay the invention of your speech on me,
    And the performance too; I'll play my part   230
    That you shall say Nature yields more than Art.

ALPHONSO.

    Be't so resolv'd; unartificial truth
    An unfeign'd passion can decipher best.

VINCENTIO.

    But 'twill be hard, my lord, for one unlearn'd.

MEDICE.

    Unlearn'd? I cry you mercy, sir. Unlearn'd?   235

VINCENTIO.

    I mean untaught, my lord, to make a speech
    As a pretended actor, without clothes
    More gracious than your doublet and your hose.

ALPHONSO.

    What, think you, son, we mean t'express a speech
    Of special weight without a like attire?   240

VINCENTIO.

    Excuse me then, my lord; so stands it well.

STROZZA [aside].

    H'as brought them rarely in, to pageant him.

MEDICE.

    What, think you, lord, we think not of attire?
    Can we not make us ready at this age?

STROZZA [to Medice].

    Alas, my lord, your wit must pardon his.   245

237. clothes] *Shepherd*; close *Q* .   *in Q or Parrott; "to Alphonso" Parrott*
245. S.D. *to* Medice] *Yamada; not*   *1.*

228–231.] Twitted earlier for his lack of art (education), Medice now claims that his untrained *nature* (natural ability) will excel the *scholastic wits* in both *invention* (devising) and elocution (*performance*).

235. *I . . . mercy*] I beg your pardon.

237. *clothes*] The Q spelling, *close,* a common variant, may nonetheless signal a pun on the term for the ending of a speech.

242.] Vincentio has prepared the others to make a show of Medice in his rich robes.

244.] possibly a Chapman joke on the age of the boy actors.

VINCENTIO.

I hope it will; his wit is pitiful.

STROZZA [*to* Vincentio].

I pray stand by, my lord; y'are troublesome.

VINCENTIO [*to* Strozza].

To none but you. —[*To* Medice.]   Am I to you, my lord?

MEDICE.

Not unto me.

VINCENTIO.   Why, then you wrong me, Strozza.

MEDICE.

Nay, fall not out, my lords.

STROZZA [*to* Alphonso].   May I not know   250
What your speech is, my liege?

ALPHONSO.   None but myself
And the Lord Medice.

MEDICE.   No, pray, my lord,
Let none partake with us.

ALPHONSO.   No, be assur'd.
But for another cause—a word, Lord Strozza.
[*Aside to* Strozza.]   I tell you true, I fear Lord Medice   255
Will scarce discharge the speech effectually;
As we go, therefore, I'll explain to you
My whole intent, that you may second him
If need and his debility require.

STROZZA.

Thanks for this grace, my liege.   Vincentio *overhears.*

MEDICE.   My lord, your son!   260

ALPHONSO.

Why, how now, son? Forbear. —Yet 'tis no matter;
We talk of other business, Medice.
And come, we will prepare us to our show.

---

247. S.D. *to* Vincentio] *Yamada;*   *Brereton;* "*Med.*" *Parrott.*
not in Q ; "*to* Medice" *Parrott.*   249, 250. S.P. MEDICE] Q ,
248, 249. S.P. VINCENTIO] Q ,   *Brereton;* "*Vin.*" *Parrott.*

---

246. *pitiful*] etymologically, full of pity, but really pitiable.
247. *stand by*] stand aside. Strozza and Vincentio begin a mock quarrel.
254. *cause*] matter.

STROZZA, VINCENTIO [*aside*].

Which, as we can, we'll cast to overthrow.   *Exeunt.*

[I.ii] *Enter* Lasso, Bassiolo, Sarpego, *two* Pages; Bassiolo *bare before.*

BASSIOLO.

Stand by there; make place.

LASSO.

Say now, Bassiolo, you on whom relies
The general disposition of my house
In this our preparation for the duke,
Are all our officers at large instructed   5
For fit discharge of their peculiar places?

BASSIOLO.

At large, my lord, instructed.

LASSO.

Are all our chambers hung? Think you our house
Amply capacious to lodge all the train?

BASSIOLO.

Amply capacious, I am passing glad.   10

LASSO.

And now, then, to our mirth and musical show
Which after supper we intend t'endure,
Welcome's chief dainties: for choice cates at home
Ever attend on princes, mirth abroad.
Are all parts perfect?

---

264. S.D. *Exeunt*] Q (*overrun above the line*); *Parrott interprets it as an exit for the other characters and adds a separate exit for Strozza and Vincentio.* [I.ii]
0.1. Lasso, Bassiolo] *Parrott; "Lasso, Corteza, Margaret, Bassiolo" Q*.

11. S.P. LASSO] *Shepherd; not in Q or Parrott; Yamada assigns to Lasso the words* I . . . glad (*l. 10*) *as well.*
12. endure] Q (indure); *induce Yamada (following a Bradley conjecture reported favorably by Parrott); Q is intelligible, but* endue *could be correct.*

---

264. *cast*] contrive, perhaps with a pun on *-throw*.
[I.ii]
0.1. *bare*] bareheaded, as required by his office.
5. *at large*] fully. The gentleman usher had authority over other household officers; see Appendix C.
8. *hung*] decorated with tapestries or arms.
10. *passing*] very.
13. *dainties . . . cates*] delicacies.

SARPEGO.   One I know there is.   15

LASSO.

    And that is yours.

SARPEGO.   Well guess'd, in earnest, lord.

    I need not *erubescere* to take

    So much upon me: that my back will bear.

BASSIOLO.

    Nay, he will be perfection itself

    For wording well and dexterous action too.   20

LASSO.

    And will these waggish pages hit their songs?

TWO PAGES [*singing*].

    Re mi fa sol la—

LASSO.

    O, they are practicing. —Good boys, well done.—

    But where is Pogio? There y'are overshot,

    To lay a capital part upon his brain,   25

    Whose absence tells me plainly he'll neglect him.

BASSIOLO.

    O no, my lord, he dreams of nothing else

    And gives it out in wagers he'll excel;

    And see, I told your lordship, he is come.

Enter Pogio.

POGIO.

    How now, my lord, have you borrowed a suit for me? —   30

    Signor Bassiolo, can all say? Are all things ready? The duke

    is hard by, and little thinks that I'll be an actor, i'faith.

    —I keep all close, my lord.

LASSO.

    O, 'tis well done. —Call all the ladies in.—

    Sister and daughter, come, for God's sake come;   35

    Prepare your courtliest carriage for the duke.

---

    17. *erubescere*] blush.

    20. *wording*] speaking his part.

    21. *hit*] succeed with.

    25. *capital*] leading.

    28. *gives . . . wagers*] gambles that. "It was common at this time to act a
part for a wager" (Parrott).

    31. *say*] speak their parts.

    33. *close*] secret.

    36. *carriage*] deportment.

Enter Corteza, Margaret, *and maids.*

CORTEZA.

 And niece, in any case remember this:
 Praise the old man, and when you see him first,
 Look me on none but him, smiling and lovingly.
 And then, when he comes near, make 'beisance low   40
 With both your hands thus moving, which not only
 Is as 'twere courtly and most comely too,
 But speaks as who should say, "Come hither, duke,"
 And yet says nothing but you may deny.

LASSO.

 Well taught, sister.

MARGARET.   Ay, and to much end: 45
 I am exceeding fond to humor him.

LASSO.

 Hark, does he come with music? What, and bound?
 An amorous device; daughter, observe.

Enter Enchanter, *with spirits singing; after them* Medice, *like* Sylvanus;
next the Duke *bound,* Vincentio, Strozza, *with others.*

VINCENTIO [*aside to* Strozza].

 Now let's gull Medice. I do not doubt
 But this attire, put on, will put him out.   50

STROZZA [*aside to* Vincentio].

 We'll do our best to that end; therefore mark.

ENCHANTER.

 Lady or princess, both your choice commands,
 These spirits and I, all servants of your beauty,
 Present this royal captive to your mercy.

MARGARET.

 Captive to me, a subject?

VINCENTIO.   Ay, fair nymph,   55
 And how the worthy mystery befell,

36.1. Margaret] *Shepherd; "Margarite" Q*.

 39. *me*] by my advice, or for me (Abbott, §220).
 43. *as who*] as if one.
 44. *but*] but what.
 46. *exceeding fond*] very foolish.
 49. *gull*] make a fool of (by rattling him just before he must speak).
 50. *out*] "at a loss from failure of memory or self-possession" (*OED*).
 52. *both . . . commands*] either title is within your choice: lady, as you already are, or princess, as you might be by marrying the duke.

Sylvanus here, this wooden god, can tell.

ALPHONSO [*to* Medice].

Now, my lord.

VINCENTIO [*to* Medice]. Now is the time, man, speak.

MEDICE.

Peace.

ALPHONSO. Peace, Vincentio.

VINCENTIO.   'Swounds, my lord,

Shall I stand by and suffer him to shame you?—   60

My Lord Medice!

STROZZA.   Will you not speak, my lord?

MEDICE.

How can I?

VINCENTIO.   But you must speak, in earnest.—

Would not your highness have him speak, my lord?

MEDICE.

Yes, and I will speak, and perhaps speak so

As you shall never mend. I can, I know.   65

VINCENTIO.

Do, then, my good lord.

ALPHONSO.   Medice, forth.

MEDICE.

Goddess, fair goddess, for no less—no less—   [*He stammers.*]

ALPHONSO.

"No less, no less"? No more, no more! —[*To* Strozza.]

Speak you.

MEDICE [*aside*].

'Swounds, they have put me out.

VINCENTIO [*to* Margaret].   Laugh you, fair goddess;

This nobleman disdains to be your fool.

ALPHONSO.   Vincentio, peace.   70

VINCENTIO.

'Swounds, my lord, it is as good a show.—

Pray speak, Lord Strozza.

69. you] *Shepherd;* your *Q.*   69. goddess;] *this edn.*; goddesle, *Q* ;
                                        goddess? *Parrott.*

57. *wooden god*] Sylvanus was god of the woods, but Vincentio is punning
on the woodenness of Medice's wit.

60. *shame you*] i.e., by representing Alphonso's cause badly.

65. *mend*] (1) improve upon (my speech), (2) recover (a threat).

STROZZA.   Honorable dame—

VINCENTIO.

    Take heed you be not out, I pray, my lord.

STROZZA.

    I pray forbear, my Lord Vincentio.—

    How this distressed prince came thus enthrall'd   75

    I must relate with words of height and wonder:

    His grace this morning visiting the woods

    And straying far to find game for the chase,

    At last out of a myrtle grove he rous'd

    A vast and dreadful boar so stern and fierce   80

    As if the fiend, fell Cruelty herself,

    Had come to fright the woods in that strange shape.

ALPHONSO [aside].

    Excellent good.

VINCENTIO [aside].   Too good, a plague on him.

STROZZA.

    The princely savage being thus on foot

    Tearing the earth up with his thundering hoof,   85

    And with th'enrag'd Aetna of his breath

    Firing the air and scorching all the woods,

    Horror held all us huntsmen from pursuit.

    Only the duke, incens'd with our cold fear,

    Encourag'd like a second Hercules—   90

VINCENTIO [aside to Strozza].

    'Swounds, too good, man.

STROZZA [to Vincentio].   Pray thee, let me alone.—

86. breath] *Shepherd*; breath. *Q*.

---

    75. *came*] came to be.

    76. *of height*] i.e., in the grand rhetorical style. What follows is parodic of romantic conventions and slyly satirical of Alphonso.

    79. *myrtle grove*] The myrtle was sacred to Venus and an emblem of love. Perhaps more to the point, it was in a myrtle grove that Adonis roused the boar that killed him (Shakespeare, *Venus and Adonis*, ll. 865 ff.).

    84. *on foot*] in motion.

    85–87.] conventional imagery for boars; cf. Ovid's account of Meleager (*Metamorphoses* VIII.272 ff.).

    89. *incens'd with*] incited to action by.

    90. *Encourag'd*] inspired with courage.

And like the English sign of great St. George—

VINCENTIO [*aside*].

Plague of that simile!

STROZZA.

Gave valorous example and, like fire,
Hunted the monster close and charg'd so fierce   95
That he enforc'd him, as our sense conceiv'd,
To leap for soil into a crystal spring,
Where on the sudden strangely vanishing,
Nymph-like for him out of the waves arose
Your sacred figure, like Diana arm'd,   100
And, as in purpose of the beast's revenge,
Discharg'd an arrow through his highness' breast,
Whence yet no wound or any blood appear'd.
With which the angry shadow left the light,
And this enchanter with his power of spirits   105
Brake from a cave, scattering enchanted sounds
That struck us senseless, while in these strange bands
These cruel spirits thus enchain'd his arms
And led him captive to your heavenly eyes,
Th'intent whereof on their report relies.   110

---

92. *English . . . George*] St. George is the patron of England, and his banner (a red cross on a white field) would lead English soldiers to valorous battle. But the *sign* of St. George slaying the dragon would also have been taken as a reference to a tavern or inn, perhaps even a bawdyhouse, identified by such a sign (Brereton); cf. Shakespeare, *King John*, II.i. 288–290.

95. *Hunted . . . close*] pressed hard after.

96. *enforc'd*] compelled.

97. *soil*] "A pool or stretch of water, used as a refuge by a hunted . . . animal" (*OED*).

99. *for him*] in place of him.

100. *like Diana arm'd*] Diana, goddess of the hunt and (like Margaret in Strozza's fiction) hostile to men, was armed with bow, quiver, and arrows; it is presumably a conscious irony that a Diana's arrow should inflict Alphonso with a Cupid's wound.

104. *With which*] at which time.

104. *angry shadow*] the "figure" (l. 100), which now disappeared.

105. *power*] fighting force.

107. *bands*] bonds.

110. *Th'intent . . . relies*] i.e., they (the spirits) will have to say why they have done so.

ENCHANTER.

    Bright nymph, that boar figur'd your cruelty,

    Chared by love, defended by your beauty.

    This amorous huntsman here we thus enthrall'd

    As the attendants on your grace's charms

    And brought him hither, by your bounteous hands   115

    To be releas'd or live in endless bands.

LASSO.

    Daughter, release the duke. —Alas, my liege,

    What meant your highness to endure this wrong?

CORTEZA.

    Enlarge him, niece; come, dame, it must be so.

MARGARET.

    What, madam, shall I arrogate so much?   120

LASSO.

    His highness' pleasure is to grace you so.

ALPHONSO.

    Perform it then, sweet love; it is a deed

    Worthy the office of your honor'd hand.

MARGARET.

    Too worthy, I confess, my lord, for me

    If it were serious; but it is in sport,   125

    And women are fit actors for such pageants.

                      [*She releases* Alphonso's *bonds.*]

ALPHONSO.

    Thanks, gracious love. Why made you strange of this?

    I rest no less your captive than before,

    For, me untying, you have tied me more.—

    Thanks, Strozza, for your speech. —[*To* Medice.]   No

        thanks to you.   130

MEDICE.

    No, thank your son, my lord.

112. Chared] *Q* ; Chased *Shepherd*;
Charged *Parrott (Bradley conjecture)*.

111. *figur'd*] represented.
112. *Chared*] driven away.
119. *Enlarge*] release; as usual when Corteza speaks, there is also a sexual
implication, to cause an erection.
127. *made you strange*] did you pretend coyness.
128. *rest*] remain.

LASSO.   'Twas very well,
Exceeding well performed on every part.—
How say you, Bassiolo?

BASSIOLO.   Rare, I protest, my lord.

CORTEZA.

    O, my Lord Medice became it rarely;
    Methought I lik'd his manly being out: 135
    It becomes noblemen to do nothing well.

LASSO.

    Now then, will't please your grace to grace our house
    And still vouchsafe our service further honor?

ALPHONSO.

    Lead us, my lord; we will your daughter lead.

                   Exit [with all but Vincentio *and* Strozza].

VINCENTIO [aside].

    You do not lead, but drag her leaden steps.   140

STROZZA.

    How did you like my speech?

VINCENTIO.   O fie upon't,
    Your rhetoric was too fine.

STROZZA.   Nothing at all;
    I hope St. George's sign was gross enough.
    But, to be serious, as these warnings pass
    Watch you your father, I'll watch Medice,   145
    That in your love-suit we may shun suspect,
    To which end, with your next occasion urge
    Your love to name the person she will choose
    By whose means you may safely write or meet.

VINCENTIO.

    That's our chief business; and see, here she comes.   150

                Enter Margaret *in haste.*

---

    133. *protest*] declare.
    134. *became it rarely*] was very apt for the occasion.
    135–136.] Corteza thinks Medice's incapacity a manly fault, but traditionally noblemen were expected to do everything not only well but effortlessly. From Corteza's lips, *manly being out* also has bawdy undertones.
    140. *lead . . . leaden*] the *-ea-* in each word was pronounced like the *-a-* in *laden.*
    143. *gross*] obvious, crude.
    146. *shun suspect*] avoid suspicion.

MARGARET.

    My lord, I only come to say y'are welcome

    And so must say farewell.

VINCENTIO.   One word, I pray.

MARGARET.

    What's that?

VINCENTIO.   You needs must presently devise

    What person trusted chiefly with your guard

    You think is aptest for me to corrupt   155

    In making him a mean for our safe meeting.

MARGARET.

    My father's usher, none so fit

    If you can work him well. And so farewell—

    With thanks, my good Lord Strozza, for your speech.   *Exit.*

STROZZA.

    I thank you for your patience, mocking lady.   160

VINCENTIO.

    O, what a fellow has she pick'd us out!

    One that I would have choos'd past all the rest.

    For his close stockings only.

STROZZA.   And why not

    For the most constant fashion of his hat?

VINCENTIO.

    Nay then, if nothing must be left unspoke,   165

    For his strict form, thus still to wear his cloak.

STROZZA.

    Well, sir, he is your own, I make no doubt,

---

   156. *mean*] means.

   163. *close*] tightly fitting, perhaps of silk, popular among gallants for showing off the "comeliness of the wearer's leg" (Linthicum, p. 261). Bassiolo dresses modishly, not, I think, in the old-fashioned manner indicated by Parrott.

   164.] i.e., he changes his hats to keep up with the styles, or perhaps the allusion is to his constant doffing of his hat (see Introduction, p. xxx).

   166. *still*] always. How Bassiolo wore his cloak is not clear, but there were modes in this as in other articles of men's attire. Because *The Gentleman Usher* was probably a Blackfriars play, one is tempted to apply to this passage the following description: "The long cloak was draped over the left shoulder half-falling, and would 'ne'er keep on', so that the gentleman who went to Blackfriars and rose between the acts could, gracefully and without apparent intention, let fall his cloak from his shoulders displaying his rich suit" (Linthicum, p. 194).

   167. *your own*] your man.

For to these outward figures of his mind
He hath two inward-swallowing properties
Of any gudgeons: servile avarice   170
And overweening thought of his own worth,
Ready to snatch at every shade of glory;
And therefore, till you can directly board him,
Waft him aloof with hats and other favors
Still as you meet him.

VINCENTIO.   Well, let me alone;   175
He that is one man's slave is free from none.   *Exeunt.*

Finis Actus Primi.

[II.i]   *Enter* Medice, Corteza, [*and*] *a page with a cup of sack.*

MEDICE.

Come, lady, sit you here. —Page, fill some sack.—
[*Aside.*]   I am to work upon this aged dame
To glean from her if there be any cause,
In loving others, of her niece's coyness
To the most gracious love-suit of the duke.—   5
Here, noble lady, this is healthful drink
After our supper.

CORTEZA.   O, 'tis that, my lord,
That of all drinks keeps life and soul in me.   [*She drinks.*]

MEDICE.

Here, fill it, page, for this my worthy love.—

                                    [*Embraces her lightly.*]
[*Aside.*]   O, how I could embrace this good old widow.   10

[II.i]   *following close"* Q. *See Introduction,*
0.1. *sack*] Parrott; "*Secke, Strozza*   p. xii.

168.] i.e., his clothes mirror his mental attitudes.
169–170. *inward-swallowing . . . gudgeons*] qualities that make gullible
people swallow (believe) anything. A gudgeon was a small bait-fish often
used to represent credulous people.
173–174.] Till you can make a direct approach, woo him with gifts
of hats, etc. The language is nautical: to *waft* is to guide a ship; *aloof* is
into the wind, away from the dangerous shoals onto which the wind
might carry it.
175. *Still as*] whenever.
[II.i]
4. *In . . . others*] by reason of Margaret's having other lovers.

CORTEZA.

    Now, lord, when you do thus, you make me think

    Of my sweet husband; for he was as like you,

    E'en the same words and fashion, the same eyes,

    Manly, and choleric, e'en as you are, just,

    And e'en as kind as you for all the world.   15

MEDICE.

    O, my sweet widow, thou dost make me proud.

CORTEZA.

    Nay, I am too old for you.

MEDICE.   Too old, that's nothing.

    Come pledge me, wench, for I am dry again

    And straight will charge your widowhood fresh, i'faith.

                               [*She drinks.*]

    Why, that's well done.

CORTEZA.   Now fie on't, here's a draught.   20

                             [*She drinks deeply.*]

MEDICE.

    O, it will warm your blood; if you should sip,

    'Twould make you heart-burn'd.

CORTEZA.   Faith, and so they say.

    Yet I must tell you, since I plied this gear

    I have been haunted with a whoreson pain here,

    And every moon almost with a shrewd fever,   25

    And yet I cannot leave it; for thank God

    I never was more sound of wind and limb.

    Enter Strozza [*as* Corteza *holds out*] *a great bombasted leg;*

                  [Strozza *eavesdrops.*]

    Look you, I warrant you I have a leg

    Holds out as handsomely—

---

    14. *choleric*] having choler as the dominant humor; hence, passionate, irascible.

    14. *just*] exactly.

    17.] Corteza interprets *proud* (l. 16) as meaning lecherous, in heat.

    18. *pledge me*] drink to me.

    22. *heart-burn'd*] (1) afflicted with cardialgia; (2) jealous or unhappy.

    23. *plied this gear*] started using this stuff (drink); *gear* also referred to the sexual organs (though the earliest citation in the *OED* is from 1675).

    25. *shrewd*] vexatious.

    27.1 *bombasted*] stuffed with cotton wool; the reference is to a stage prop.

    29. *Holds . . . handsomely*] that is still well formed.

MEDICE.   Beshrew my life,
But 'tis a leg indeed, a goodly limb.   30
STROZZA [*aside*].
    This is most excellent.
MEDICE.   O, that your niece
    Were of as mild a spirit as yourself.
CORTEZA.
    Alas, Lord Medice, would you have a girl
    As well seen in behavior as I?
    Ah, she's a fond young thing, and grown so proud   35
    The wind must blow at west still or she'll be angry.
MEDICE.
    Mass, so me thinks. How coy she's to the duke!
    I lay my life she has some younger love.
CORTEZA.
    Faith, like enough.
MEDICE.   Gods me, who should it be?
CORTEZA.
    If it be any—page, a little sack—   40
    If it be any—hark now—if it be,
    I know not, by this sack, but if it be,
    Mark what I say, my lord—I drink t'ye first.
MEDICE.
    Well said, good widow; much good do thy heart.   [*She drinks.*]
    So. Now what if it be?
CORTEZA.   Well, if it be,   45
    To come to that I said, for so I said,
    If it be any, 'tis the shrewd young prince,
    For eyes can speak and eyes can understand,
    And I have mark'd her eyes. Yet, by this cup,
    Which I will only kiss—   [*She drinks.*]

37. thinks] *Parrott*; thinke *Q* .

---

32. *mild*] yielding.

34. *well . . . behavior*] "well versed in courtly manners" (Parrott).

36.] she must always have her way; the west wind was proverbially associated with good weather (Tilley, W 445).

37. *Mass*] by the mass, a mild oath.

37. *me thinks*] it seems to me.

39. *Gods me*] God save me, a mild oath.

44. *much . . . heart*] a toast.

STROZZA [*aside*].   O noble crone,   50
    Now such a huddle and kettle never was.

CORTEZA.
    I never yet have seen, not yet I say,
    But I will mark her after for your sake.

MEDICE.
    And do, I pray, for it is passing like;
    And there is Strozza, a sly counsellor   55
    To the young boy: O, I would give a limb
    To have their knavery limn'd and painted out.
    They stand upon their wits and paper-learning;
    Give me a fellow with a natural wit
    That can make wit of no wit, and wade through   60
    Great things with nothing when their wits stick fast.
    O, they be scurvy lords.

CORTEZA.   Faith, so they be;
    Your lordship still is of my mind in all,
    And e'en so was my husband.

MEDICE [*seeing* Strozza].   Gods my life,
    Strozza hath eavesdropp'd here and overheard us.   65

STROZZA [*aside*].
    They have descried me. —[*Coming forward.*] What, Lord
      Medice,
    Courting the lusty widow?

MEDICE.   Ay, and why not?
    Perhaps one does as much for you at home.

STROZZA.
    What, choleric, man? and toward wedlock too?

CORTEZA.
    And if he be, my lord, he may do worse.   70

---

51. *huddle and kettle*] confused mess (*OED* cites this passage).

54. *passing like*] very likely.

55. *there*] merely an expletive, but it might have been staged with Strozza
reacting as though he has been seen.

57. *limn'd . . . out*] portrayed as in a picture so that it can be readily seen.

60. *wit . . . wit*] clever utterance . . . learning.

61. *Great . . . nothing*] important affairs as if they were nothing (or, with
their lack of formal education), contrasted with the inability of *their* wits
(educated people's, Strozza's and Vincentio's) to cope.

68.] i.e., perhaps some man is courting your wife.

70–71.] Corteza answers Strozza's first question (l. 67); Strozza then
responds as if she had answered his later questions (l. 69).

STROZZA.

> If he be not, madam, he may do better.

> *Enter* Bassiolo *with servants with rushes, and a carpet.*

BASSIOLO.

> My lords and madam, the duke's grace entreats you
> T'attend his new-made duchess for this night
> Into his presence.

STROZZA.   We are ready, sir.

> *Exeunt* [Strozza, Medice, Corteza, *and page*].

BASSIOLO.

> Come, strew this room afresh; spread here this carpet.   75
> Nay, quickly, man, I pray thee. This way, fool:
> Lay me it smooth and even. Look if he will!
> This way a little more, a little there.
> Hast thou no forecast? 'Slud, methinks a man
> Should not of mere necessity be an ass.—   80
> Look how he strows here too. Come, Sir Giles Goosecap,
> I must do all myself; lay me 'em thus,
> In fine smooth threaves, look you, sir, thus in threaves.
> Perhaps some tender lady will squat here,
> And if some standing rush should chance to prick her,   85

---

73. *new-made . . . night*] Margaret; see ll. 180–185.

75. *strew*] with clean rushes. "The floor of the Blackfriars stage, like the floors of contemporary cottages and palaces all over England, was strewn with rushes" (Smith, p. 318).

75. *carpet*] although "carpets normally served as coverings for tables and chests rather than for floors, [this carpet was] spread upon the stage" (Smith, p. 321).

79. *forecast*] design, plan (*OED*), possibly punning on forward throw.

80. *mere necessity*] anglicizing of the theological Latin term *mera necessitas*, absolute predestination.

81. *Sir Giles Goosecap*] foolish titular hero of another Chapman comedy (see Introduction, pp. xiv–xv); *goosecap*, goose's head, was a common term for a dolt.

83. *threaves*] bundles tied like small sheaves. Bassiolo seems to be using the word strangely: *OED* cites this as the earliest usage in this sense; its older meanings were, literally, two shocks of corn or, figuratively, a large number. In l. 112, Vincentio seems surprised by Bassiolo's use of the word.

85. *standing . . . prick*] The phallic pun is obvious, but perhaps not to Bassiolo: foolish characters were often made victims of their own unconscious bawdry.

She'd squeak and spoil the songs that must be sung.

Enter Vincentio *and* Strozza.

STROZZA [*aside to* Vincentio].

    See where he is; now to him, and prepare

    Your familiarity.

VINCENTIO [*coming forward*]. Save you, Master Bassiolo;

    I pray, a word, sir—but I fear I let you.

BASSIOLO.

    No, my good lord, no let.   [*He removes his hat.*]

VINCENTIO.   I thank you, sir.   90

    Nay, pray be cover'd; O, I cry you mercy

    You must be bare.

BASSIOLO.   Ever to you, my lord.

VINCENTIO.

    Nay, not to me, sir,

    But to the fair right of your worshipful place.

                              [*He removes his hat.*]

STROZZA [*aside*].

    A shame of both your worships.   [*Exit.*]

BASSIOLO.   What means your lordship? 95

VINCENTIO.

    Only to do you right, sir, and myself ease.

    And what, sir, will there be some show tonight?

BASSIOLO.

    A slender presentation of some music

    And something else, my lord.

VINCENTIO.   'Tis passing good, sir.

    I'll not be overbold t'ask the particulars.   100

BASSIOLO.

    Yes, if your lordship please.

86.1 *Enter . . .* Strozza] *Parrott; after*   95. S.D. *Exit*] *Parrott 1*; *not in* Q ;
familiaritie (1. *88*) *in* Q .   *after* lordship *in Parrott.*

    89. *let*] hinder.

    91. *be cover'd*] put your hat on.

    91–94.] Vincentio acknowledges that the gentleman usher must remove his hat by virtue of his office, denying the need to do so in honor of Vincentio.

    95. *worships*] ironic, since the gentleman usher was not entitled to the term.

    96.] Vincentio has removed his hat, he says, out of respect for the gentleman usher and to be comfortable.

VINCENTIO.   O no, good sir,
    But I did wonder much, for as methought
    I saw your hands at work.
BASSIOLO.   Or else, my lord,
    Our business would be but badly done.
VINCENTIO.
    How virtuous is a worthy man's example!   105
    Who is this throne for, pray?
BASSIOLO.   For my lord's daughter,
    Whom the duke makes to represent his duchess.
VINCENTIO.
    'Twill be exceeding fit; and all this room
    Is passing well prepar'd: a man would swear
    That all presentments in it would be rare.   110
BASSIOLO [to a servant].
    Nay, see if thou canst lay 'em thus, in threaves.
VINCENTIO.
    In threaves, d'ye call it?
BASSIOLO.   Ay, my lord, in threaves.
VINCENTIO.
    A pretty term.
    Well, sir, I thank you highly for this kindness
    And pray you always make as bold with me   115
    For kindness more than this, if more may be.
BASSIOLO.
    O, my lord, this is nothing.
VINCENTIO.   Sir, 'tis much.
    And now I'll leave you, sir; I know y'are busy.
BASSIOLO.
    Faith, sir, a little.
VINCENTIO.   I commend me t'ye, sir.   *Exit* Vincentio.
BASSIOLO [aside].
    A courteous prince, believe it; I am sorry   120

---

103. *hands*] meant figuratively in the first instance, but perhaps literally
as well; Bassiolo takes only the literal sense.

105. *virtuous*] powerful.

106. *throne*] Courtly entertainments were characteristically staged in
halls having an area (the "state") from which, seated in a chair, or *throne*,
the monarch or guest of honor watched the performance.

110. *presentments*] presentations.

110. *rare*] exceptional, perhaps meant ambiguously.

I was no bolder with him. What a phrase
He us'd at parting! "I commend me t'ye."
I'll ha't, i'faith.

Enter Sarpego *half-dress'd.*

SARPEGO.

Good master usher, will you dictate to me
Which is the part precedent of this nightcap   125
And which posterior? I do *ignorare*
How I should wear it.

BASSIOLO.   Why, sir, this, I take it,
Is the precedent part; ay, so it is.

SARPEGO.

And is all well, sir, think you?

BASSIOLO.   Passing well.

Enter Pogio *and* Fungus.

POGIO [*to* Fungus].

Why, sir, come on; the usher shall be judge.—   130
See, master usher: this same Fungus here,
Your lord's retainer, whom I hope you rule,
Would wear this better jerkin for the rush-man,
When I do play the broom-man and speak first.

FUNGUS.

Why, sir, I borrowed it, and I will wear it.   135

POGIO.

What, sir, in spite of your lord's gentleman usher?

FUNGUS.

No spite, sir, but you have chang'd twice already
And now would ha't again.

POGIO.   Why, that's all one, sir:
Gentility must be fantastical.

---

122. *I . . . t'ye*] apparently a currently fashionable phrase, perhaps even
one identified with some individual; the imitation of such phrases was
often satirized (see Wilhelm Creizenach, *The English Drama in the Age of
Elizabeth,* tr. Cécile Hugon [London, 1916], p. 328). See V.i.82–83.

126. *ignorare*] not know.

133–134. *rush-man . . . broom-man*] sellers of rushes (*OED*) and of brooms
(Parrott).

138. *that's all one*] that makes no difference.

139. *Gentility*] members of the gentry.

BASSIOLO.

    I pray thee, Fungus, let master Pogio wear it.   140

FUNGUS.

    And what shall I wear then?

POGIO.   Why, here is one

    That was a rush-man's jerkin, and I pray,

    Were't not absurd then a broom-man should wear it?

FUNGUS.

    Faugh, there's a reason. I will keep it, sir.

POGIO.

    Will, sir? —Then do your office, master usher: 145

    Make him put off his jerkin; you may pluck

    His coat over his ears, much more his jerkin.

BASSIOLO.

    Fungus, y'ad best be rul'd.

FUNGUS.   Best, sir! I care not.

POGIO.

    No, sir? I hope you are my lord's retainer;

    I need not care a pudding for your lord.   150

    But spare not; keep it, for perhaps I'll play

    My part as well in this as you in that.

BASSIOLO.

    Well said, master Pogio; my lord shall know it.

Enter Corteza, *with the broom-wench and rush-wench in their petticoats, cloaks over them, with hats over their head-'tires.*

CORTEZA.

    Look, master usher, are these wags well dress'd?

    I have been so in labor with 'em, truly.   155

BASSIOLO.

    Y'ave had a very good deliverance, lady.—

    [*Aside.*]   How I did take her at her labor there!

    I use to gird these ladies so sometimes.

---

140. thee] *Q corr.*; the *Q uncorr.*   154. usher] *Q corr.* (Vsher);
148. sir!] *Q corr.*; sir, *Q uncorr.*   "*Superintendent*" *Q uncorr.*

    146–147. *pluck . . . ears*] discharge him (strip him of his livery).

    149–150.] Fungus owes allegiance to Lasso (*my lord*) and, hence, obedience to Lasso's gentleman usher; Pogio, not a servant, owes nothing to Lasso (*your lord*).

    158. *use to gird*] am accustomed to gibe at.

Enter Lasso *with [a] sylvan and a nymph, a man bug and a woman [bug].*

FIRST MASQUER.

    I pray, my lord, must not I wear this hair?

LASSO.

    I pray thee, ask my usher. —Come, dispatch;   160
    The duke is ready; are you ready there?

SECOND MASQUER.

    See, master usher: must he wear this hair?

FIRST BUG.

    Pray, master usher, where must I come in?

SECOND BUG.

    Am not I well for a bug, master usher?

BASSIOLO.

    What stir is with these boys here! God forgive me,   165
    If 'twere not for the credit on't, I'd see
    Your apish trash afire ere I'd endure this.

FIRST MASQUER.

    But pray, good master usher—

BASSIOLO.   Hence, ye brats.
    You stand upon your 'tire, but for your action
    Which you must use in singing of your songs   170
    Exceeding dexterously and full of life,

158.1. *a sylvan]* this edn.; "*Syluan*" *Q* ; Sylvanus *Parrott*.

158.1. *woman bug] Parrott;* "*woman*" *Q* .

159. S.P. FIRST MASQUER] *this edn.*; 1 *Q* ; "*1st Bug*" *Parrott;* "*Syluan*" *Yamada. Yamada's assignments of this speech and of l. 162 are appealing for their efficient use of the characters who entered in l. 158.1, and would likely have been made in a prompt-copy; but to an author in the act of writing it does not matter much which minor character says which of these lines, and I have assumed that Chapman, mainly concerned to show an air of pre-performance con-*

fusion under Bassiolo's direction, did not trouble to specify the speakers. Under these circumstances, any editorial specification would be arbitrary.

162. S.P. SECOND MASQUER] *this edn.*; 2 *Q* ; "*2nd Bug*" *Parrott;* "*Nymph*" *Yamada.*

162. *usher] Q corr.* (Vsher); "*Superintendent*" *Q uncorr.*

163. S.P. FIRST BUG] *Q* (1. *Bug*); "*Man Bug*" *Yamada.*

164. S.P. SECOND BUG] *Parrott;* 2 *Q* ; "*Woman Bug*" *Yamada.*

168. S.P. FIRST MASQUER] *this edn.*; 1 *Q* ; "*1st Bug*" *Parrott;* "*Man Bug*" *Yamada*

158.1 *sylvan]* a woodland spirit.

158.1 *bug]* bugbear.

169. *stand . . . 'tire]* fuss about your costumes.

I hope you'll then stand like a sort of blocks
Without due motion of your hands and heads
And wresting your whole bodies to your words.
Look to't, y'are best, and in. Go, all go in.   175

POGIO.

Come in, my masters; let's be out anon.

Exeunt [all except Lasso *and* Bassiolo].

LASSO.

What, are all furnish'd well?

BASSIOLO.   All well, my lord.

LASSO.

More lights, then, here, and let loud music sound.

BASSIOLO.

Sound music.

Exeunt.

[*Music sounds.*] *Enter* Vincentio, Strozza *bare*, Margaret, Corteza, *and*
Cynanche *bearing her train. After her the* Duke *whispering with* Medice,
Lasso *with* Bassiolo, *&c.*

ALPHONSO.

Advance yourself, fair duchess, to this throne,   180
As we have long since rais'd you to our heart.
Better decorum never was beheld
Than 'twixt this state and you; and as all eyes
Now fix'd on your bright graces think it fit,
So frame your favor to continue it.   185

MARGARET [*seating herself on the throne*].

My lord, but to obey your earnest will
And not make serious scruple of a toy,
I scarce durst have presum'd this minute's height.

---

172. *hope*] suppose.

173. *due*] appropriate. Anthony Caputi thinks this passage shows the
child actors' exaggerated acting style caricaturing adult actors (*John
Marston, Satirist* [Ithaca, 1961], p. 104).

182. *decorum*] appropriateness; the term was commonly used in dramatic
criticism.

183. *state*] (1) the area of the hall in which the principal guests sat, and
(2) her status as Alphonso's duchess.

185.] be gracious enough to occupy this throne permanently (as my
duchess).

187. *toy*] game.

188.] "I would hardly have presumed to take the high position, i.e. the
throne, or chair of state, which I now fill for a moment" (Parrott).

LASSO.

    Usher, cause other music; begin your show.

BASSIOLO.

    Sound, consort. Warn the pedant to be ready.   190

                                        [*Music changes.*]

CORTEZA.

    Madam, I think you'll see a pretty show.

CYNANCHE.

    I can expect no less in such a presence.

ALPHONSO.

    Lo, what attention and state beauty breeds,

    Whose moving silence no shrill herald needs.

Enter Sarpego.

SARPEGO.   195

    Lords of high degree

    And ladies of low courtesy,

    I the pedant here,

    Whom some call schoolmastere,

    Because I can speak best

    Approach before the rest.   200

VINCENTIO.

    A very good reason.

SARPEGO.

    But there are others coming

    Without mask or mumming,

    For they are not ashamed,

    If need be, to be named,   205

    Nor will they hide their faces

    In any place or places;

194. moving] *Shepherd*; moning *Q*.

---

190. *Sound, consort*] Play, musicians.

194. *moving . . . needs*] *moving* is probably an adjective modifying *silence*,
but could be a gerund having *silence* as object; either way, as Parrott notes,
"the sense is about the same, i.e. 'Beauty needs no herald'" to command
attention to itself. Cf. the proverbial "Where Beauty is there needs no
other plea" (Tilley, B 177).

196. *low*] obeisant.

203. *mumming*] disguise for a mummers' play.

For though they seem to come
Loaded with rush and broom,
The broom-man, you must know,   210
Is signor Pogio,
Nephew, as shall appear,
To my lord Strozza here—

STROZZA.

O Lord! I thank you, sir; you grace me much.

SARPEGO.

And to this noble dame,   215
Whom I with finger name.   [*Gesturing toward* Cynanche.]

VINCENTIO.

A plague of that fool's finger!

SARPEGO.

And women will ensue
Which, I must tell you true,
No women are indeed   220
But pages made, for need,
To fill up women's places
By virtue of their faces
And other hidden graces.
A hall, a hall; whist, still, be mum,   225
For now with silver song they come.

Enter Pogio [*as broom-man and*] Fungus [*as rush-man*] *with the song;
broom-maid and rush-maid. After which* Pogio [*speaks*].

POGIO.

Heroes and heroines of gallant strain,
Let not these brooms motes in your eyes remain;

215. S.P. SARPEGO] *Shepherd; not in*
Q.

216.] In view of Vincentio's reaction (l. 217), perhaps Sarpego's "finger"
points obscenely; but possibly Vincentio is merely objecting, as Strozza
just did, to having Pogio's family relationship to Cynanche publicly
identified.

222. *places*] (1) roles, (2) sexual organs.

225. *A hall, a hall*] the cry used to clear a space and to ask for silence.

226.1. *with the song*] as the song is sung. Such songs between acts were
characteristic of plays performed by the children's companies.

For in the moon there's one bears wither'd bushes,
But we, dear wights, do bear green brooms, green rushes,   230
Whereof these verdant herbals cleped broom
Do pierce and enter every lady's room.
And to prove them high-born and no base trash,
Water with which your phys'nomies you wash
Is but a broom; and, more truth to deliver,   235
Grim Hercules swept a stable with a river.
The wind that sweeps foul clouds out of the air
And for you ladies makes the welkin fair
Is but a broom. And O dan Titan bright,
Most clerkly call'd the scavenger of night,   240
What art thou but a very broom of gold,
For all this world not to be cried nor sold?
Philosophy, that passion sweeps from thought,
Is the soul's broom and by all brave wits sought;
Now if philosophers but broom-men are,   245
Each broom-man then is a philosopher.
And so we come, gracing your gracious graces,
To sweep care's cobwebs from your cleanly faces.

ALPHONSO.
    Thanks, good master broom-man.
FUNGUS.   For me, rush-man, then
    To make rush ruffle in a verse of ten: 250
    A rush which now your heels do lie on here—

VINCENTIO.
    Cry mercy, sir.

229.] "The spots in the moon, according to a very old popular belief,
represent a man with a bundle of sticks" (Parrott).

230. *wights*] people.

231. *herbals*] bunches of plants (*OED*, citing this as a nonce usage). The usual
senses are (1) a book about plants, and (2) a collection of plant specimens.

231. *cleped*] called.

234. *phys'nomies*] physiognomies, faces.

236.] Hercules cleaned the Augean stable, his fifth labor, by diverting
two rivers through it.

238. *welkin*] sky.

240. *Most clerkly call'd*] as the clerks (scholars) call it.

240. *scavenger of night*] i.e., because it cleans away the night.

242. *cried*] hawked for sale (as real brooms are).

250. *rufflle . . . ten*] swagger in decasyllabic verse.

252.] Vincentio ironically apologizes for resting his feet on the floor-
covering rushes.

FUNGUS.

> Was whilom used for a pungent spear
> In that odd battle, never fought but twice,
> As Homer sings, betwixt the frogs and mice.   255
> Rushes make true-love knots, rushes make rings;
> Your rush, maugre the beard of winter, springs.
> And when with gentle, amorous, lazy limbs
> Each lord with his fair lady sweetly swims
> On these cool rushes, they may with these bables   260
> Cradles for children make, children for cradles.
> And lest some Momus here might now cry, "Push,"
> Saying our pageant is not worth a rush,
> Bundles of rushes, lo, we bring along
> To pick his teeth that bites them with his tongue.   265

STROZZA.

> See, see, that's Lord Medice.

VINCENTIO [*to* Medice].   Gods me, my lord,
> Has he pick'd you out picking of your teeth?

MEDICE.

> What pick you out of that?

STROZZA.   Not such stale stuff
> As you pick from your teeth.

ALPHONSO.   Leave this war with rushes.—

---

253. *whilom*] once upon a time.

253–255.] In the Greek mock-heroic poem *Batrachomyomachia*, traditionally thought to be by Homer, the frogs used sharp bulrushes for spears in an unsuccessful battle against the mice. Fungus is wrong in saying that the battle was *never fought but twice,/ As Homer sings*, for there is only one general battle in the poem. Could Chapman be alluding satirically to some recent translation which he considered so loose as to constitute a new telling of the story, and therefore a second battle? A translation by W[illiam] F[owldes] was published in 1603 in which the translator admitted that he had not "word for word concurd with the Author" (sig. Blv). Chapman translated the poem too, but surely much later (printed c. 1624).

256. *true-love knots*] ornamental knots, usually of two loops intertwined, symbolic of lovers.

257. *maugre the beard*] despite the snow.

260. *bables*] baubles, toys.

262. *Momus*] captious critic (from Momus, god of ridicule).

262. *Push*] pish.

265. *bites . . . tongue*] ridicules them.

Good master pedant, pray, forth with your show.   270

SARPEGO.

 Lo, thus far then, brave duke, you see
 Mere entertainment; now our glee
 Shall march forth in morality,
 And this quaint duchess here shall see
 The fault of virgin nicety   275
 First wooed with rural courtesy.—
 Disburden them. —Prance on this ground,
 And make your exit with your round.

       [*Broom- and rush-players dance and*] *exeunt.*

 Well have they danc'd, as it is meet,
 Both with their nimble heads and feet.   280
 Now, as our country girls held off
 And rudely did their lovers scoff,
 Our nymph likewise shall only glance
 By your fair eyes and look askance
 Upon her feral friend that woos her,   285
 Who is in plain field forc'd to lose her.

   [*Enter sylvan and nymph, who dance and exeunt.*]

 And after them, to conclude all,
 The purlieu of our pastoral:
 A female bug and eke her friend
 Shall only come and sing, and end.   290

[*Enter man-bug and woman-bug, who sing the*] *bugs' song* [*and exeunt.*]

269–270. rushes. . . . pedant,] *in l. 289.*
Parrott; Rushes, . . . pedant; *Q* . 289. female] *Q* . *corr*.; Femall *Q*
285. feral] *Parrott* (*Bradley conjec-* *uncorr.*
ture); female *Q* . *Cf. the press-variant*

---

 272. *glee*] play, entertainment.
 273. *morality*] the *utile* (didactic) to go with the *dulce* (*Mere entertainment*, l. 272) and thus satisfy the Horatian requirement for poetry. Yamada suggests that the subject of the following dances was the pursuit of Syrinx by Pan.
 274. *quaint*] beautiful.
 275. *nicety*] coyness.
 277. *Disburden them*] take their burden (of brooms and rushes).
 285. *feral*] untamed.
 288. *purlieu*] limit, i.e., conclusion.

This, lady and duchess, we conclude:
Fair virgins must not be too rude;
For though the rural wild and antic
Abus'd their loves as they were frantic,
Yet take you in your ivory clutches   295
This noble duke and be his duchess.
Thus, thanking all for their *tacete*,
I void the room and cry *valete*.   *Exit.*

ALPHONSO.

Generally well and pleasingly performed.

MARGARET [*rising*].

Now I resign this borrowed majesty,   300
Which sat unseemly on my worthless head,
With humble service to your highness' hands.

[*She gives her crown to* Alphonso.]

ALPHONSO.

Well you became it, lady, and I know
All here could wish it might be ever so.

STROZZA [*aside*].

Here's one says nay to that.

VINCENTIO [*aside to* Strozza].   Plague on you, peace!   305

LASSO.

Now let it please your highness to accept
A homely banquet to close these rude sports.

ALPHONSO.

I thank your lordship much.

BASSIOLO.   Bring lights; make place.

Enter Pogio *in his cloak and broom-man's attire.*

POGIO.

How d'ye, my lord.

ALPHONSO.

O, master broom-man, you did passing well.   310

VINCENTIO.

Ah, you mad slave, you! You are a tickling actor.

291. This] Q *text*; Thus Q *catch-*
word, Parrott.

---

297. *tacete*] silence (literally, be silent).
298. *void*] leave.
298. *valete*] farewell.
311. *tickling*] pleasing.

POGIO.

    I was not out like my Lord Medice.—

    How did you like me, aunt?

CYNANCHE.   O, rarely, rarely.

STROZZA.

    O, thou hast done a work of memory

    And rais'd our house up higher by a story.   315

VINCENTIO [*aside to* Cynanche].

    Friend, how conceit you my young mother here?

CYNANCHE [*aside to* Vincentio].

    Fitter for you, my lord, than for your father.

VINCENTIO [*aside to* Cynanche].

    No more of that, sweet friend; those are bugs' words.   *Exeunt.*

Finis Actus Secundi.

[III.i]   Medice, *after the song, whispers alone with his* Servant.

MEDICE.

    Thou art my trusty servant, and thou know'st

    I have been ever bountiful lord to thee,

    As still I will be. Be thou thankful, then,

    And do me now a service of import.

SERVANT.

    Any, my lord, in compass of my life.   5

MEDICE.

    Tomorrow, then, the duke intends to hunt,

    Where Strozza, my despiteful enemy,

    Will give attendance busy in the chase;

    Wherein, as if by chance, when others shoot

    At the wild boar, do thou discharge at him   10

    And with an arrow cleave his canker'd heart.

SERVANT.

    I will not fail, my lord.

III.i.] See Appendix D.

---

    316. *how conceit you*] what do you think of. The "young mother," of course, is Margaret, intended to be Alphonso's wife.

    318. *bugs' words*] i.e., frightening because Alphonso might hear (Parrott), or painfully true.

[III.i]

    0.1. *song*] see II.i.226.1, note.

MEDICE.   Be secret, then,
      And thou to me shalt be the dear'st of men.   *Exeunt.*

[III.ii]   *Enter* Vincentio *and* Bassiolo [*separately*].

VINCENTIO [*aside*].
      Now vanity and policy enrich me
      With some ridiculous fortune on this usher.—
      Where's master usher?
BASSIOLO.   Now I come, my lord.
VINCENTIO.
      Besides, good sir, your show did show so well—
BASSIOLO.
      Did it indeed, my lord?
VINCENTIO.   O sir, believe it: 5
      'Twas the best-fashion'd and well-order'd thing
      That ever eye beheld; and therewithal
      The fit attendance by the servants us'd,
      The gentle guise in serving every guest
      In other entertainments, everything   10
      About your house so sortfully dispos'd
      That, even as in a turnspit call'd a jack
      One vice assists another, the great wheels
      Turning but softly make the less to whir
      About their business, every different part   15
      Concurring to one commendable end,
      So and in such conformance, with rare grace,
      Were all things order'd in your good lord's house.
BASSIOLO.
      The most fit simile that ever was.
VINCENTIO.
      But shall I tell you plainly my conceit   20
      Touching the man that I think caus'd this order?

[III.ii]
      1. *vanity . . . policy*] Bassiolo's vanity and Vincentio's policy (cunning).
      4. *Besides*] besides the fact that. After an interruption, Vincentio carries on with this sentence at l. 8.
      11. *sortfully*] in an appropriate manner (*OED*, citing only this passage).
      12. *turnspit . . . jack*] "A machine for turning the spit in roasting meat" (*OED*).
      13. *vice*] screw or cog.
      21. *Touching*] concerning.

BASSIOLO.

    Ay, good my lord.

VINCENTIO.   You note my simile.

BASSIOLO.

    Drawn from the turnspit.

VINCENTIO.   I see you have me:

    Even as in that quaint engine you have seen

    A little man in shreds stand at the winder   25

    And seems to put all things in act about him,

    Lifting and pulling with a mighty stir,

    Yet adds no force to it nor nothing does,

    So, though your lord be a brave gentleman

    And seems to do this business, he does nothing;   30

    Some man about him was the festival robe

    That made him show so glorious and divine.

BASSIOLO.

    I cannot tell, my lord; yet I should know

    If any such there were.

VINCENTIO.   Should know, quoth you?

    I warrant you know. Well, some there be   35

    Shall have the fortune to have such rare men,

    Like brave beasts to their arms, support their state,

    When others of as high a worth and breed

    Are made the wasteful food of them they feed.

    What state hath your lord made you for your service?   40

BASSIOLO.

    He has been my good lord, for I can spend

    Some fifteen hundred crowns in lands a year,

---

    23. *have*] understand.

    25. *little man*] a dummy fastened to the handle as though he were activating the *engine*, which is actually wound up and run by clockwork. The tenor of the simile is that Lasso is the *little man* and Bassiolo the activating power.

    29. *brave*] finely dressed; the shifted image grows out of the little man *in shreds* (l. 25).

    31. *festival robe*] especially colorful costume.

    37. *brave beasts*] colorful heraldic animals (lions, bears, etc.) on coats of arms.

    42. *fifteen . . . lands*] income from lands worth £375 (capital value). The gentlemen ushers of the English royal court earned £30 per year. A *crown* is five shillings (one-fourth of a pound). See Appendix C.

Which I have gotten since I serv'd him first.

VINCENTIO.

No more than fifteen hundred crowns a year?

BASSIOLO.

It is so much as makes me live, my lord,   45
Like a poor gentleman.

VINCENTIO.   Nay, 'tis pretty well;
But certainly my nature does esteem
Nothing enough for virtue, and had I
The duke my father's means, all should be spent
To keep brave men about me. But good sir,   50
Accept this simple jewel at my hands
Till I can work persuasion of my friendship
With worthier arguments.

BASSIOLO.   No, good my lord;
I can by no means merit the free bounties
You have bestowed besides.

VINCENTIO.   Nay, be not strange,   55
But do yourself right and be all one man
In all your actions. Do not think but some
Have extraordinary spirits like yourself
And will not stand in their society
On birth and riches, but on worth and virtue,   60
With whom there is no niceness nor respect
Of others' common friendship. Be he poor
Or basely born, so he be rich in soul
And noble in degrees of qualities,
He shall be my friend sooner than a king.   65

BASSIOLO.

'Tis a most kingly judgment in your lordship.

---

54. *free*] free-handed, suggesting that Vincentio has followed Strozza's advice (I.ii.174).

59–62. *And . . . friendship*] and rely (*stand*) on worth and virtue rather than on class and wealth in choosing their personal associations (*society*); such people have no fastidiousness (*niceness*) or concern over what their ordinary "friends" will think. The thought is consistent with views expressed in other Chapman plays, but is here being used ironically by Vincentio.

64. *degrees of qualities*] rank based on personal merit rather than on birth.

VINCENTIO.

 Faith, sir, I know not, but 'tis my vain humor.

BASSIOLO.

 O, 'tis an honor in a nobleman.

VINCENTIO.

 Y'ave some lords now so politic and proud

 They scorn to give good looks to worthy men.   70

BASSIOLO.

 O, fie upon 'em. By that light, my lord,

 I am but servant to a nobleman,

 But if I would not scorn such puppet lords,

 Would I were breathless.

VINCENTIO.   You, sir? So you may,

 For they will cog so when they wish to use men 75

 With "pray be cover'd, sir," "I beseech you, sit,"

 "Who's there? wait of master usher to the door."

 O, these be godly gudgeons. Where's the deeds?

 The perfect nobleman?

BASSIOLO.   O, good my lord—

VINCENTIO.

 Away, away! Ere I would flatter so,   80

 I would eat rushes like Lord Medice.

BASSIOLO.

 Well, well, my lord, would there were more such princes.

VINCENTIO.

 Alas, 'twere pity, sir: they would be gull'd

 Out of their very skins.

---

74. were] *Shepherd*; weare *Q* .   81. Medice] *Shepherd*; *Medici Q* .

---

 67. *humor*] whim.

 71. *light*] candle; the children performed their plays indoors, unlike many performances by adult companies.

 75. *cog*] deceive. Bassiolo does not recognize that Vincentio is describing his own "policy."

 77. *Who's . . . of*] Someone, escort.

 78. *godly gudgeons*] fine baits.

 81. *eat rushes*] use a toothpick. With the repeated references to Medice's picking his teeth, cf. Shakespeare's *All's Well*, I.i.171–172: "like the brooch and the tooth-pick, which wear not now." One can envision a staging in which Vincentio catches Bassiolo about to pick his teeth with a rush; Bassiolo's "Well, well" (l. 82) sounds like a temporizing, flustered answer.

BASSIOLO.

Why, how are you, my lord?

VINCENTIO.   Who, I? I care not: 85
If I be gull'd where I profess plain love,
'Twill be their faults, you know.

BASSIOLO.   O, 'twere their shames.

VINCENTIO.

Well, take my jewel; you shall not be strange.
I love not many words.

BASSIOLO [taking the jewel].   My lord, I thank you.
I am of few words too.

VINCENTIO.   'Tis friendly said;   90
You prove yourself a friend, and I would have you
Advance your thoughts and lay about for state
Worthy your virtues: be the minion
Of some great king or duke. There's Medice,
The minion of my father—O, the Father!   95
What difference is there! But I cannot flatter:
A word to wise men.

BASSIOLO.   I perceive your lordship.

VINCENTIO.

"Your lordship"? Talk you now like a friend?
Is this plain kindness?

BASSIOLO.   Is it not, my lord?

VINCENTIO.

A palpable flatt'ring figure for men common: 100
O' my word I should think, if 'twere another,
He meant to gull me.

BASSIOLO.   Why, 'tis but your due.

---

94. Medice] *Shepherd*; *Medici Q*.   *Parrott*.
96. there!] *this edn.*; there? *Q*,   96. flatter:] *Shepherd*; flatter *Q*.

---

85. *how are you*] how are you gulled.

89. *I love . . . words*] Many Renaissance dramatic characters bent on mischief profess to be men of few words. Cf. the proverb "Truth (Plain dealing) has no need of rhetoric" (Tilley, T 575).

92. *Advance your thoughts*] think of yourself in higher terms.

92. *lay . . . state*] plan for a station in life.

95–96. *O . . . difference*] oh God! what a difference.

100. *figure . . . common*] mode of address fit only for common men (Parrott).

VINCENTIO.

   'Tis but my due if you'll be still a stranger,
   But as I wish to choose you for my friend,
   As I intend, when God shall call my father,　　　　105
   To do I can tell what—but let that pass;
   Thus 'tis not fit—let my friend be familiar:
   Use not me "lordship," nor yet call me lord,
   Nor my whole name, Vincentio, but Vince,
   As they call Jack or Will. 'Tis now in use　　　　110
   'Twixt men of no equality or kindness.

BASSIOLO.

   I shall be quickly bold enough, my lord.

VINCENTIO.

   Nay, see how still you use that coy term "lord";
   What argues this but that you shun my friendship?

BASSIOLO.

   Nay, pray say not so.

VINCENTIO.　　　　　　　　Who should not say so?　　　　115
   Will you afford me now no name at all?

BASSIOLO.

   What should I call you?

VINCENTIO.　　　　　　　　Nay, then, 'tis no matter.
   But I told you: Vince.

BASSIOLO.　　　　　　　　Why, then, my sweet Vince.

VINCENTIO.

   Why, so then. And yet still there is a fault
   In using these kind words without kind deeds:　　　　120
   Pray thee, embrace me too.

BASSIOLO.　　　　　　　　　Why then, sweet Vince.
　　　　　　　　　　　　　　　[*He embraces* Vincentio.]

VINCENTIO.

   Why, now I thank you. 'Sblood, shall friends be strange?
   Where there is plainness, there is ever truth,
   And I will still be plain since I am true.
   Come, let us lie a little; I am weary.　　　　125

108. me] *Q* ; my *Parrott.*

---

103. *still*] always.
108. *Use not me*] do not use for me.
111. *kindness*] kinship.
125. *lie*] a pun, growing out of *true*, l. 124.

BASSIOLO.

And so am I, I swear, since yesterday.   [*They lie down together.*]

VINCENTIO.

You may, sir, by my faith. And sirrah, hark thee,
What lordship wouldst thou wish to have, i'faith,
When my old father dies?

BASSIOLO.   Who, I? Alas!

VINCENTIO.

O, not you! Well, sir, you shall have none.   130
You are as coy a piece as your lord's daughter.

BASSIOLO.

Who, my mistress?

VINCENTIO.   Indeed, is she your mistress?

BASSIOLO.

Ay, faith, sweet Vince, since she was three year old.

VINCENTIO.

And are not we too friends?

BASSIOLO.   Who doubts of that?

VINCENTIO.

And are not two friends one?

BASSIOLO.   Even man and wife.   135

VINCENTIO.

Then what to you she is, to me she should be.

BASSIOLO.

Why, Vince, thou wouldst not have her?

VINCENTIO.   O, not I;
I do not fancy anything like you.

BASSIOLO.

Nay, but I pray thee, tell me.

VINCENTIO.

You do not mean to marry her yourself?   140

BASSIOLO.

Not I, by heaven.

VINCENTIO.   Take heed now, do not gull me.

BASSIOLO.

No, by that candle.

134. too] *Q* ; two *all other edns.*

---

132. *mistress . . . mistress*] superior . . . paramour. See Appendix C.
135.] orthodox Renaissance doctrine: see L. J. Mills, *One Soul in Bodies Twain* (Bloomington, 1937).

VINCENTIO.   Then will I be plain:

    Think you she dotes not too much on my father?

BASSIOLO.

    O yes, no doubt on't.

VINCENTIO.   Nay, I pray you, speak.

BASSIOLO.

    You seely man, you, she cannot abide him.   145

VINCENTIO.

    Why, sweet friend, pardon me; alas, I knew not.

BASSIOLO.

    But I do note you are in some things simple

    And wrong yourself too much.

VINCENTIO.   Thank you, good friend.

    For your plain dealing, I do mean so well.

BASSIOLO.

    But who saw ever summer mix'd with winter?   150

    There must be equal years where firm love is.

    Could we two love so well so suddenly

    Were we not something equaller in years

    Than he and she are?

VINCENTIO.   I cry ye mercy, sir.

    I know we could not, but yet be not too bitter,   155

    Considering love is fearful. And sweet friend,

    I have a letter t'entreat her kindness,

    Which if you would convey—

BASSIOLO.   Ay, if I would, sir?

VINCENTIO.

    Why, faith, dear friend, I would not die requiteless.

BASSIOLO.

    Would you not so, sir?   160

    By heaven, a little thing would make me box you.

    "Which if you would convey"? Why not, I pray,

    "Which, friend, thou shalt convey"?

VINCENTIO.   Which, friend, you shall then.

---

145. *seely*] silly.

163. *thou shalt . . . you shall*] the distinction in forms here may be meaningless, for it was generally breaking down, but *thou* was still the form usually used for "(1) affection towards friends, (2) good-humoured superiority to servants, and (3) contempt or anger to strangers" (Abbott, §231).

BASSIOLO.

Well, friend, and I will then.

VINCENTIO.

And use some kind persuasive words for me?   165

BASSIOLO.

The best, I swear, that my poor tongue can forge.

VINCENTIO.

Ay, well said, "poor tongue"; O, 'tis rich in meekness.
You are not known to speak well? You have won
Direction of the earl and all his house,
The favor of his daughter and all dames   170
That ever I saw come within your sight,
With a poor tongue? A plague o' your sweet lips.

BASSIOLO.

Well, we will do our best; and faith, my Vince,
She shall have an unwieldy and dull soul
If she be nothing mov'd with my poor tongue—   175
Call it no better; be it what it will.

VINCENTIO.

Well said, i'faith. Now if I do not think
'Tis possible, besides her bare receipt
Of that my letter with thy friendly tongue,
To get an answer of it, never trust me.   180

BASSIOLO.

An answer, man? 'Sblood, make no doubt of that.

VINCENTIO.

By heaven, I think so. Now a plague of Nature
That she gives all to some and none to others.

BASSIOLO [aside].

How I endear him to me! —Come, Vince, rise.   [They rise.]
Next time I see her, I will give her this,   185
Which when she sees she'll think it wondrous strange
Love should go by descent and make the son
Follow the father in his amorous steps.

VINCENTIO.

She needs must think it strange, that never yet saw
I durst speak to her or had scarce her sight.   190

---

183. *all*] i.e., all the talents (to Bassiolo).

BASSIOLO.

    Well, Vince, I swear thou shalt both see and kiss her.

VINCENTIO.

    Swears my dear friend? By what?

BASSIOLO.   Even by our friendship.

VINCENTIO.

    O sacred oath! which how long will you keep?

BASSIOLO.

    While there be bees in Hybla or white swans

    In bright Meander, while the banks of Po   195

    Shall bear brave lilies, or Italian dames

    Be called the bona-robas of the world.

VINCENTIO.

    'Tis elegantly said; and when I fail,

    Let there be found in Hybla hives no bees,

    Let no swans swim in bright Meander stream   200

    Nor lilies spring upon the banks of Po,

    Nor let one fat Italian dame be found

    But lean and brawn-fall'n, ay, and scarcely sound.

BASSIOLO.

    It is enough; but let's embrace withal.

VINCENTIO.

    With all my heart.   [*They embrace.*]

BASSIOLO.   So; now farewell, sweet Vince.   *Exit.* 205

VINCENTIO.

    Farewell, my worthy friend. —I think I have him.

Enter Bassiolo.

BASSIOLO [*aside*].

    I had forgot the parting phrase he taught me.—

    I commend me t'ye, sir.   *Exit instanter.*

---

194. *Hybla*] a Sicilian district famous for its honey.

194–195. *swans . . . Meander*] The swans in the river Meander, in Asia Minor, are Ovidian, but *bright* is scarcely apt for the Meander, which has always been noted for its muddiness.

197. *bona-robas*] "as we say, good stuffe, a good wholesome plum-cheeked wench" (Florio); "A wench; 'a showy wanton'" (*OED*, citing Samuel Johnson). This conclusion to Bassiolo's series is ridiculously anti-climactic.

203. *brawn-fall'n*] "shrunken in flesh, thin, skinny" (*OED*).

203. *sound*] healthy, often used with reference to venereal disease.

208. S.D. *instanter*] immediately (literally, vehemently).

VINCENTIO.   At your wish'd service, sir.—
O fine friend, he had forgot the phrase:
How serious apish souls are in vain form.   210
Well, he is mine, and he being trusted most
With my dear love may often work our meeting,
And being thus engag'd dare not reveal.

Enter Pogio *in haste*, Strozza *following.*

POGIO.

Horse, horse, horse, my lord, horse; your father is going a-
hunting.   215

VINCENTIO.

My lord horse? You ass, you, d'ye call my lord horse?

STROZZA.

Nay, he speaks huddles still; let's slit his tongue.

POGIO.

Nay, good uncle, now; 'sblood, what captious merchants
you be. So the duke took me up even now; my lord uncle
here and my old Lord Lasso, by heaven y'are all too witty 220
for me: I am the veriest fool on you all, I'll be sworn.

VINCENTIO.

Therein thou art worth us all, for thou know'st thyself.

STROZZA.

But your wisdom was in a pretty taking last night, was it
not, I pray?

POGIO.

O, for taking my drink a little? I'faith, my lord, for that 225
you shall have the best sport presently with Madam Corteza
that ever was; I have made her so drunk that she does
nothing but kiss my Lord Medice. See, she comes riding
the duke; she's passing well mounted, believe it.

212. love] *Shepherd*; ioue *Q* .

---

217. *huddles*] confusion (*OED*, citing this passage).
218. *merchants*] fellows.
219. *took me up*] interrupted me reprovingly (*OED*).
221. *on*] of (Abbott).
223. *pretty taking*] fine condition.
228. *riding*] leaning on (with sexual overtones).
229. *mounted*] (1) as if she were "riding" a horse, (2) sexually aroused.

Enter Alphonso, Corteza [*leaning on him,* Margaret], Cynanche, Bassiolo *first, two women attendants, and Huntsmen,* Lasso, [*and* Medice. Strozza *and* Vincentio *remain apart from the others.*]

ALPHONSO.

Good wench, forbear.   230

CORTEZA.

My lord, you must put forth yourself among ladies; I warrant you have much in you if you would show it: see, a cheek o' twenty, the body of a George, a good leg still, still a good calf and not flabby nor hanging, I warrant you, a brawn of a thumb here and 'twere a pull'd partridge. —Niece 235 Meg, thou shalt have the sweetest bedfellow on him that ever call'd lady husband; try him, you shamefac'd bauble, you, try him.

MARGARET.

Good madam, be rul'd.

CORTEZA.

What a nice thing it is, my lord; you must set forth this 240 gear and kiss her, i'faith you must: get you together and be naughts awhile, get you together.

ALPHONSO.

Now, what a merry harmless dame it is!

CORTEZA.

My Lord Medice, you are a right noble man and will do a woman right in a wrong matter and need be. Pray do you 245

229.1. *leaning . . .* Margaret] *Parrott* (*ess.*); *not in* Q.
229.2. *and* Medice] *Yamada* (*ess.*); *not in* Q.
229.3. Strozza . . . *others*] *this edn.*; *not in* Q. *Cf. III.ii.286.2–3, and note that Strozza and Vincentio are not* addressed (*except in a reading deleted from l. 276*).
234. flabby] *Shepherd*; slabby Q (*defended by Brereton as a Yorkshire dialect word meaning slight in construction, thin*).

233. *o' twenty*] i.e., of a twenty-year-old.

233. *a George*] a St. George.

235. *thumb*] on one level, penis; several other words in her speech also have bawdy implications (*put forth yourself, much in you,* etc.).

235. *and*] if.

240–241. *set . . . gear*] "take this business in hand" (Parrott); on another level, show this sexual organ.

242. *be naughts*] be quiet and withdraw (*OED*, citing this passage), but *naughts* suggests *naughty*.

give the duke ensample upon me: you come a-wooing to me
now; I accept it.

LASSO.

What mean you, sister?

CORTEZA [*to* Lasso].

Pray, my lord, away. —[*To* Medice.]   Consider me as I
am, a woman.   250

POGIO [*aside*].

Lord, how I have whittl'd her!

CORTEZA.

You come a-wooing to me now. —Pray thee, duke, mark
my Lord Medice—and do you mark me, virgin. —[*Moving
from one to another.*]   Stand you aside, my lord—all—and
you, give place. —Now, my Lord Medice, put case I be 255
strange a little, yet you like a man put me to it. Come kiss
me, my lord; be not asham'd.

MEDICE.

Not I, madam, I come not a-wooing to you.

CORTEZA.

'Tis no matter, my lord. Make as though you did, and come
kiss me; I won't be strange a whit.   260

LASSO.

Fie, sister, y'are to blame; pray, will you go to your chamber?

CORTEZA.

Why, hark you, brother.

LASSO.

What's the matter?

CORTEZA.

D'ye think I am drunk?

LASSO.

I think so truly.   265

CORTEZA.

But are you sure I am drunk?

LASSO.

Else I would not think so.

261. to blame] *Shepherd*; too blame *Q* .

---

246. *ensample*] example.
251. *whittl'd*] made drunk.
255. *put case*] suppose.
256. *put . . . it*] make me comply.

CORTEZA.

But I would be glad to be sure on't.

LASSO.

I assure you then.

CORTEZA.

Why then, say nothing and I'll be gone;   270

God b'w'y', lord. —Duke, I'll come again anon.   *Exit.*

LASSO.

I hope your grace will pardon her, my liege,

For 'tis most strange: she's as discreet a dame

As any in these countries and as sober

But for this only humor of the cup.   275

ALPHONSO.

'Tis good, my lord, sometimes.—

Come, to our hunting; now 'tis time, I think.

OMNES.

The very best time of the day, my lord.

ALPHONSO.

Then my lord, I will take my leave till night,

Reserving thanks for all my entertainment   280

Till I return. —In meantime, lovely dame,

Remember the high state you last presented,

And think it was not a mere festival show,

But an essential type of that you are

In full consent of all my faculties.—   285

And hark you, good my lord—

[Alphonso *whispers with* Lasso.] Medice *whispers with* First Huntsman
all this while. Vincentio *and* Strozza *have all this while talked together a*
pretty way. [*Others converse apart.*]

VINCENTIO [*aside to* Strozza].   See now, they whisper

276. sometimes] Q *corr.*; sometimes: *beside l. 297 in* Q .
Soune [*i.e., son*] and my Lords Q   286.2–3. Vincentio . . . *way*]   *Shep-*
uncorr. See Introduction, p. xiii *and n. 6.*   *herd; beside ll. 282–285 in* Q .
286.1–2. Medice . . . *while*] *this edn.*;   286.3 *Others . . . apart*] see l. 289 *n.*

284–285. *that . . . consent*] that which you are, by the unanimous agreement.

286.1–3. *Alphonso . . . way*] I have bunched Q's scattered stage directions
to convey an impression of what now happens: several whispered conversa-
tions are occurring simultaneously, of which we hear parts of each in turn.
A pretty way means a considerable time.

Some private order, I dare lay my life,
For a forc'd marriage 'twixt my love and father.
I therefore must make sure, and noble friends,
I'll leave you all when I have brought you forth   290
And seen you in the chase. Meanwhile observe,
In all the time this solemn hunting lasts,
My father and his minion Medice,
And note if you can gather any sign
That they have miss'd me and suspect my being,   295
If which fall out send home my page before.

STROZZA [aside to Vincentio].

I will not fail, my lord.

MEDICE [aside to First Huntsman]. Now take thy time.

FIRST HUNTSMAN [aside to Medice].

I warrant you, my lord, he shall not 'scape me.

ALPHONSO [to Margaret].

Now, my dear mistress, till our sports intended
End with my absence, I will take my leave.   300

LASSO.

Bassiolo, attend you on my daughter.

          Exeunt [Alphonso, Lasso, Pogio, Medice, and Huntsmen].

BASSIOLO.

I will, my lord.

VINCENTIO [aside to Strozza].

Now will the sport begin. I think my love

298. S.P. FIRST HUNTSMAN] *Parrott*;
"*Hunt.*" *Q* .

---

289. *friends*] If this is not merely an error for *friend*, perhaps Vincentio is
addressing Alphonso and Medice ironically and *sotto voce*. Parrott assumed
that Cynanche, at least, has joined Strozza and Vincentio for this whispered
conversation; strictly speaking, however, she will not be "in the chase," and
her Farewell (l. 305) suggests that she has been with Margaret, who is
apparently not with Vincentio (see l. 303). Bassiolo and Pogio, not "noble
friends," are unaccounted for and may be with the women attendants
until Bassiolo joins Margaret, apparently at l. 302.

292. *solemn hunting*] formal hunting party (Parrott).

295. *my being*] my whereabouts (Parrott).

296. *fall out*] occur.

297. *take*] choose.

299–300. *our . . . absence*] i.e., my absence from here will end as soon as
the hunting party ends.

Will handle him as well as I have done.

Exit [Vincentio *and* Strozza].

CYNANCHE.

Madam, I take my leave and humbly thank you.   305

MARGARET.

Welcome, good madam. —Maids, wait on my lady.

Exit [Cynanche *with women attendants*].

BASSIOLO.

So, mistress, this is fit.

MARGARET.   Fit, sir? Why so?

BASSIOLO.

Why so? I have most fortunate news for you.

MARGARET.

For me, sir? I beseech you, what are they?

BASSIOLO.

Merit and Fortune, for you, both agree;   310

Merit what you have, and have what you merit.

MARGARET.

Lord, with what rhetoric you prepare your news!

BASSIOLO.

I need not, for the plain contents they bear,

Utter'd in any words, deserve their welcome,

And yet I hope the words will serve the turn.   315

[*He produces* Vincentio's *letter.*]

MARGARET.

What, in a letter?

BASSIOLO.   Why not?

MARGARET.   Whence is it?

BASSIOLO.

From one that will not shame it with his name,

And that is Lord Vincentio.

MARGARET.   King of heaven!

Is the man mad?

BASSIOLO.   Mad, madam? Why?

MARGARET.

O heaven, I muse a man of your importance   320

Will offer to bring me a letter thus!

---

317. *that . . . name*] whose name is a credit to the letter.

BASSIOLO.

    Why, why, good mistress, are you hurt in that?
    Your answer may be what you will yourself.

MARGARET.

    Ay, but you should not do it. Gods my life,
    You shall answer it.

BASSIOLO.   Nay, you must answer it.   325

MARGARET.

    I answer it! Are you the man I trusted?
    And will betray me to a stranger thus?

BASSIOLO.

    That's nothing, dame: all friends were strangers first.

MARGARET.

    Now was there ever woman overseen so
    In a wise man's discretion?   330

BASSIOLO.

    Your brain is shallow. Come, receive this letter.

MARGARET.

    How dare you say so, when you know so well
    How much I am engaged to the duke?

BASSIOLO.

    The duke? A proper match, a grave old gent'man:
    Has beard at will and would, in my conceit,   335
    Make a most excellent pattern for a potter
    To have his picture stamp'd on a jug
    To keep ale-knights in memory of sobriety.
    Here, gentle madam, take it.

MARGARET.   Take it, sir?
    Am I common taker of love letters?   340

BASSIOLO.

    Common? Why, when receiv'd you one before?

MARGARET.

    Come, 'tis no matter. I had thought your care

340. common] *Q* ; a common *all
other edns.*

   329–330. *overseen . . . discretion*] so much mistaken in believing in a wise
man's discretion.

   335. *Has . . . will*] is old enough to grow a beard as he wishes.

   338. *ale-knights*] drunkards (who would be frightened out of their
drinking habits by the picture).

Of my bestowing would not tempt me thus
To one I know not, but it is because
You know I dote so much on your direction.   345

BASSIOLO.

On my direction?

MARGARET.   No, sir, not on yours.

BASSIOLO.

Well, mistress, if you will take my advice
At any time, then take this letter now.

MARGARET.

'Tis strange. I wonder the coy gentleman,
That seeing me so oft would never speak,   350
Is on the sudden so far rapt to write.

BASSIOLO.

It show'd his judgment that he would not speak,
Knowing with what a strict and jealous eye
He should be noted. Hold, if you love yourself.
Now will you take this letter? Pray be rul'd.   355

MARGARET [reaching for the letter].

Come, you have such another plaguey tongue.
                    [She pulls back her hand.]
And yet, i'faith, I will not.

BASSIOLO.   Lord of heaven!
What, did it burn your hands? Hold, hold, I pray,
And let the words within it fire your heart.

MARGARET.

I wonder how the devil he found you out   360
To be his spokesman. O, the duke would thank you
If he knew how you urg'd me for his son.
                    [She takes the letter and reads it.]

BASSIOLO [aside].

The duke? I have fretted her
Even to the liver, and had much ado

345.] "There is a double meaning in this line, either, 'I am so apt to
follow your advice blindly', or 'I am so dotingly fond of you'. Bassiolo
takes it in the latter sense" (Parrott).

346. *No . . . yours*] Parrott may be right in thinking this an aside.

354. *noted*] observed.

364. *liver*] thought to be the seat of love and other passions.

To make her take it, but I knew 'twas sure,   365
For he that cannot turn and wind a woman
Like silk about his finger is no man.
I'll make her answer't too.

MARGARET.   O, here's good stuff.
Hold, pray take it for your pains to bring it.

> [*She returns the letter to him.*]

BASSIOLO.

Lady, you err in my reward a little,   370
Which must be a kind answer to this letter.

MARGARET.

Nay then, i'faith, 'twere best you brought a priest
And then your client and then keep the door.
Gods me, I never knew so rude a man.

BASSIOLO.

Well, you shall answer; I'll fetch pen and paper.   *Exit.* 375

MARGARET.

Poor usher, how wert thou wrought to this brake?
Men work on one another for we women,
Nay each man on himself, and all in one
Say no man is content that lies alone.
Here comes our gulled squire.

> [*Enter* Bassiolo.]

BASSIOLO [*giving her paper*].   Here, mistress, write.   380

MARGARET.

What should I write?

BASSIOLO.   An answer to this letter.

MARGARET.

Why, sir, I see no cause of answer in it,
But if you needs will show how much you rule me,
Sit down and answer it as you please yourself.
[*Returning the paper.*]   Here is your paper; lay it fair afore
    you.   385

---

373. *keep*] keep watch at.
376. *wrought . . . brake*] worked into this trap.
378. *in one*] in one voice.
385. *fair afore*] squarely before.

BASSIOLO [*sitting down*].

    Lady, content. I'll be your secretory.

                                [*He reads* Vincentio's *letter.*]

MARGARET [*aside*].

    I fit him in this task: he thinks his pen

    The shaft of Cupid in an amorous letter.

BASSIOLO.

    Is here no great worth of your answer, say you?

    Believe it, 'tis exceedingly well writ.   390

MARGARET.

    So much the more unfit for me to answer,

    And therefore let your style and it contend.

BASSIOLO.

    Well, you shall see I will not be far short,

    Although indeed I cannot write so well

    When one is by as when I am alone.   395

MARGARET.

    O, a good scribe must write though twenty talk

    And he talk to them too.

BASSIOLO.   Well, you shall see.   [*He writes.*]

MARGARET [*aside*].

    A proper piece of scribeship, there's no doubt:

    Some words pick'd out of proclamations

    Or great men's speeches or well-selling pamphlets.   400

    See how he rubs his temples: I believe

    His muse lies in the back-part of his brain,

    Which, thick and gross, is hard to be brought forward.—

    What? Is it loath to come?

BASSIOLO.   No, not a whit.

    Pray hold your peace a little.   405

MARGARET [*aside*].

    He sweats with bringing on his heavy style.

    I'll ply him still till he sweat all his wit out.—

    What, man, not yet?

BASSIOLO.

    'Swounds, you'll not extort it from a man.

    How do you like the word *endear*?   410

388. *shaft*] arrow.
389. *Is . . . answer*] isn't this worthy of your answering it?
403. *Which*] refers to "muse."

MARGARET.

O fie upon't.

BASSIOLO.

Nay, then I see your judgment. What say you to *condole*?

MARGARET.

Worse and worse.

BASSIOLO.

O brave! I should make a sweet answer if I should use no
words but of your admittance.   415

MARGARET.

Well, sir, write what you please.

BASSIOLO.

Is *model* a good word with you?

MARGARET.

Put them together, I pray.

BASSIOLO.

So I will, I warrant you.   [*He writes.*]

MARGARET [*aside*].

See, see, see, now it comes pouring down.   420

BASSIOLO.

I hope you'll take no exceptions to *believe it.*

MARGARET.

Out upon't, that phrase is so run out of breath in trifles
that we shall have no belief at all in earnest shortly: "Believe
it, 'tis a pretty feather"; "believe it, a dainty rush"; "believe
it, an excellent cockscomb."   425

BASSIOLO.

So, so, so, your exceptions sort very collaterally.

MARGARET.

Collaterally? There's a fine word now; wrest in that if you
can by any means.

BASSIOLO [*aside*].

I thought she would like the very worst of them all. —How
think you? Do not I write and hear and talk too now?   430

---

422. *run . . . trifles*] overused for trifling matters.

425. *cockscomb*] a cap worn by the fool. Probably this last phrase was to
be taken by the audience as referring to Bassiolo.

426. *exceptions . . . collaterally*] "objections fall away from the main
point" (Parrott); or, perhaps, objections go together very badly.

MARGARET.

By my soul, if you can tell what you write now, you write
very readily.

BASSIOLO.

That you shall see straight.

MARGARET.

But do you not write that you speak now?

BASSIOLO.

O yes, do you not see how I write it? I cannot write when   435
anybody is by me, I.

MARGARET.

Gods my life, stay, man; you'll make it too long.

BASSIOLO.

Nay, if I cannot tell what belongs to the length of a lady's
device, i'faith—

MARGARET.

But I will not have it so long.   440

BASSIOLO.

If I cannot fit you—   [He is about to rise.]

MARGARET [aside].

O me, how it comes upon him! —Prithee, be short.

BASSIOLO.

Well, now I have done, and now I will read it: [reads] "Your
lordship's motive accommodating my thoughts with the very
model of my heart's mature consideration, it shall not be   445
out of my element to negotiate with you in this amorous
duello, wherein I will condole with you that our project
cannot be so collaterally made as our endeared hearts may
very well seem to insinuate—"

---

434. *that*] that which.

435–436. *I cannot . . . I*] actually a boast that his earlier judgment of himself (ll. 394–395) was inadequate. Perhaps we should read *aye* for the last *I*.

437. *stay*] stop.

439. *device*] something devised, here letter, with a double meaning.

441. *fit*] suit, with a double meaning.

443–449. *Your . . . insinuate*] This gobbledygook is barely intelligible.
Virtually every key word is a very recent innovation in English, at least in
the sense intended: e.g., *motive* (in the specific sense "a moving or inciting
cause" first cited by the *OED* in 1591), *accommodating* (1588 in this sense,
1531 earliest in any sense), *model* (1575), *element* (of non-material things,
1599), *negotiate* (1599), *duello* (1588, but in the sense here meant, "duel,"
the first citation is 1612), *condole* (1590), *endeared* (1580), *insinuate* (1579).

MARGARET.

> No more! No more! Fie upon this!   450

BASSIOLO.

> Fie upon this? He's accurs'd that has to do with these
> unsound women of judgment. If this be not good, i'faith—

MARGARET.

> But 'tis so good 'twill not be thought to come from a woman's
> brain.

BASSIOLO.

> That's another matter.   455

MARGARET.

> Come, I will write myself.

BASSIOLO.

> O' God's name, lady.—[*He rises;* Margaret *sits down and writes.*]
> [*Aside.*]   And yet I will not lose this, I warrant you; I know
> for what lady this will serve as fit. [*Pocketing his letter.*]   Now
> we shall have a sweet piece of inditement.   460

MARGARET.

> How spell you *foolish*?

BASSIOLO.

> *F-oo-l-i-s-h.*   [*Aside.*]   She   will   presume   t'indite   that
> cannot spell.

MARGARET.

> How spell you *usher*?

BASSIOLO.

> 'Sblood, you put not in those words together, do you?   465

MARGARET.

> No, not together.

BASSIOLO.

> What is betwixt, I pray?

MARGARET.

> *As the.*

BASSIOLO.

> *Ass the?* Betwixt *foolish* and *usher*? Gods my life, "foolish
> ass the usher"?   470

MARGARET.

> Nay then, you are so jealous of your wit, now read all I
> have written, I pray.

468. *As*] *Shepherd*; Asse *Q*.

---

452. *unsound . . . judgment*] women of unsound judgment cf. l. 203, *n.*

BASSIOLO [*reads*].

"I am not so foolish as the usher would make me." O, "so
foolish as the usher would make me"! —Wherein would I
make you foolish?   475

MARGARET.

Why, sir, in willing me to believe he lov'd me so well, being
so mere a stranger.

BASSIOLO.

O, is't so? You may say so indeed.

MARGARET.

Cry mercy, sir, and I will write so too.   [*After starting to
write again, she stops and rises.*]   And yet my hand is so vile; 480
pray thee, sit thee down and write as I bid thee.

BASSIOLO.

With all my heart, lady.   [*He sits down.*]   What shall I
write now?

MARGARET.

You shall write this, sir: "I am not so foolish to think you
love me, being so mere a stranger—"   485

                                    [Bassiolo *begins to write.*]

BASSIOLO.

"So mere a stranger—"

MARGARET.

"And yet I know love works strangely—"

BASSIOLO.

"Love works strangely—"

MARGARET.

"And therefore take heed by whom you speak for love—"

BASSIOLO.

"Speak for love—"   490

MARGARET.

"For he may speak for himself—"

BASSIOLO.

"May speak for himself—"

MARGARET.

"Not that I desire it—"

BASSIOLO.

"Desire it—"

477. *mere*] absolute.

MARGARET.

"But if he do, you may speed, I confess—" 495

BASSIOLO.

"Speed I confess—"

MARGARET.

"But let that pass. I do not love to discourage anybody—"

BASSIOLO.

"Discourage anybody—"

MARGARET.

"Do you, or he, pick out what you can. And so, farewell."

BASSIOLO.

"And so fare well." Is this all? 500

MARGARET.

Ay, and he may thank your siren's tongue that it is so much.

BASSIOLO [*reading over the letter*].

A proper letter, if you mark it.

MARGARET.

Well, sir, though it be not so proper as the writer, yet 'tis
as proper as the inditer. Every woman cannot be a gentleman usher; they that cannot go before must come behind. 505

BASSIOLO.

Well, lady, this I will carry instantly. I commend me t'ye,
lady. *Exit.*

MARGARET.

Pitiful usher. What a pretty sleight
Goes to the working up of everything!
What sweet variety serves a woman's wit! 510
We make men sue to us for that we wish.
Poor men, hold out a while and do not sue,
And spite of custom we will sue to you. *Exit.*

Finis Actus Tertii.

---

495. *if . . . speed*] if he (Bassiolo) desires it (to speak for himself), you
may not succeed (*speed*, normally meaning succeed, is used ironically).
Bassiolo seems oblivious to the substance of her words: he cannot write
and think simultaneously.

502. *mark*] observe.

504. *inditer*] composer.

[IV.i] *Enter* Pogio, *running in and knocking at* Cynanche's *door.*

POGIO.

    O God, how weary I am! —[*Shouts.*]   Aunt, madam,
    Cynanche, aunt!

                [*Enter* Cynanche.]

CYNANCHE.

    How now?

POGIO.   O God, aunt! O God, aunt! O God!

CYNANCHE.

    What bad news brings this man? Where is my lord?

POGIO.

    O aunt, my uncle—he's shot.

CYNANCHE.   Shot! Ay me!   5

    How is he shot?

POGIO.   Why, with a forked shaft

    As he was hunting, full in his left side.

CYNANCHE.

    O me accurs'd! Where is he? Bring me, where?

POGIO.

    Coming with Doctor Benevenius.
    I'll leave you and go tell my Lord Vincentio.   *Exit.*   10

Enter Benevenius *with others, bringing in* Strozza *with an arrow in his side.*

CYNANCHE [*aside*].

    See the sad sight! I dare not yield to grief,
    But force feign'd patience, to recomfort him.—
    My lord, what chance is this? How fares your lordship?

STROZZA.

    Wounded, and faint with anguish. —Let me rest.

BENEVENIUS.

    A chair!

CYNANCHE. O doctor, is't a deadly hurt?   15

2.1. *Enter* Cynanche] *Parrott*; *not in*
Q.
7. side.] *Q corr.*; side? *Q uncorr.*

9. Benevenius] *Yamada; Beniuemus*
Q.
10.1. Benevenius] *Yamada; Beniuemus*
Q.

---

6. *forked shaft*] barbed arrow.
12. *recomfort*] relieve.

BENEVENIUS.

    I hope not, madam, though not free from danger.

CYNANCHE.

    Why pluck you not the arrow from his side?

BENEVENIUS.

    We cannot, lady, the fork'd head so fast
    Sticks in the bottom of his solid rib.

STROZZA.

    No mean, then, doctor, rests there to educe it?   20

BENEVENIUS.

    This only, my good lord: to give your wound
    A greater orifice and in sunder break
    The pierced rib, which being so near the midriff
    And opening to the region of the heart
    Will be exceeding dangerous to your life.   25

STROZZA.

    I will not see my bosom mangled so,
    Nor sternly be anatomiz'd alive;
    I'll rather perish with it sticking still.

CYNANCHE.

    O no. —Sweet doctor, think upon some help.

BENEVENIUS.

    I told you all that can be thought in art,   30
    Which since your lordship will not yield to use,
    Our last hope rests in Nature's secret aid,
    Whose power at length may happily expel it.

STROZZA.

    Must we attend at Death's abhorred door
    The torturing delays of slavish Nature?   35
    My life is in mine own powers to dissolve,
    And why not then the pains that plague my life?—

---

23. *midriff*] diaphragm, thought to be as deadly a place for a wound as the brain, heart, or liver (*OED*).

27. *sternly be anatomiz'd*] savagely be dissected.

32. *secret*] beyond human understanding. To leave the arrowhead in would not accord with the best Renaissance medical opinion: "It is an inhumane part, and much digressing from Art, to leave the Iron in the wound. . . . it is much better to try a doubtfull remedy, than none at all" (Ambroise Paré, *Works*, tr. Th. Johnson [London, 1634], p. 439).

Rise, Furies, and this fury of my bane
Assail and conquer. What men madness call
(That hath no eye to sense but frees the soul,   40
Exempt of hope and fear, with instant fate)
Is manliest reason. —Manliest reason, then,
Resolve and rid me of this brutish life;
Hasten the cowardly protracted cure
Of all diseases. —King of physicians, Death,   45
I'll dig thee from this mine of misery.   [*He tries to rise.*]

CYNANCHE.

O hold, my lord; this is no Christian part,
Nor yet scarce manly, when your mankind foe,
Imperious Death, shall make your groans his trumpets
To summon resignation of Life's fort,   50
To fly without resistance. You must force
A countermine of fortitude, more deep
Than this poor mine of pains, to blow him up
And, spite of him, live victor though subdu'd.
Patience in torment is a valor more   55
Than ever crown'd th'Alcmenean conqueror.

47. hold,] *Shepherd*; hold *Q*.

---

38. *Furies*] He asks the goddesses of madness to remove his suffering (*bane*) by making him mad.

40. *hath . . . sense*] does not concern itself with the physical senses.

41. *instant fate*] present (immediate) determination; or perhaps present (in this life) death (to pain). In either case, the soul is freed by being released from both hope and fear.

43. *Resolve*] dissolve.

43. *brutish*] merely animal.

44. *cure*] i.e., death, which we put off in a cowardly way (*cowardly protracted*).

48. *mankind*] furious, savage.

51. *To fly*] in apposition with *this* (l. 47).

52–53. *countermine . . . mine*] Strozza has used *mine* as a place from which to dig a treasure, death. Cynanche, continuing the military image begun in l. 48, uses it as an excavation (*pains*) under the wall of a fort (*Life*) by a besieging enemy (*Death*). The *countermine* (*fortitude*) was a shaft dug by the defenders of a fort beneath the attackers' mine; a small charge placed beneath the enemy diggers destroyed them.

54. *live . . . subdu'd*] conquer death even if you die.

56. *th'Alcmenean conqueror*] Hercules, son of Alcmene.

STROZZA.

Rage is the vent of torment. Let me rise.

CYNANCHE.

Men do but cry that rage in miseries,
And scarcely beaten children become cries.
Pains are like women's clamors, which, the less   60
They find men's patience stirred, the more they cease.
Of this 'tis said, afflictions bring to God
Because they make us like him, drinking up
Joys that deform us with the lusts of sense,
And turn our general being into soul,   65
Whose actions, simply formed and applied,
Draw all our body's frailties from respect.

STROZZA.

Away with this unmed'cinable balm
Of worded breath. —[*Calming as his pain eases.*] Forbear,
    friends. Let me rest;
I swear I will be bands unto myself.   70

BENEVENIUS.

That will become your lordship best indeed.

STROZZA [*feeling the pain again*].

I'll break away and leap into the sea
Or from some turret cast me headlong down
To shiver this frail carcass into dust.

CYNANCHE.

O my dear lord, what unlike words are these   75
To the late fruits of your religious noblesse?

STROZZA.

Leave me, fond woman.

67. body's] *Shepherd*; bodies *Q*.

---

59. *scarcely . . . cries*] crying is scarcely fitting even for children who are
beaten.
66. *simply . . . applied*] "conceived and performed *simply*, i.e. apart from
physical admixture" (Parrott).
67. *Draw . . . from respect*] remove from our consideration (Parrott).
68. *unmed'cinable*] unhealing.
69. *worded*] made into words (*OED* cites this as the first use of the par-
ticiple).
70. *bands unto myself*] my own bond (not to kill himself).
76. *religious noblesse*] "pious nobility of mind," as shown in l. 70 (Parrott).

CYNANCHE.   I'll be hewn from hence
   Before I leave you. —Help me, gentle doctor.
BENEVENIUS.
   Have patience, good my lord.
STROZZA.   Then lead me in.
   Cut off the timber of this cursed shaft   80
   And let the fork'd pile canker to my heart.
CYNANCHE.
   Dear lord, resolve on humble sufferance.
STROZZA.
   I will not hear thee, woman; be content.
CYNANCHE.
   O, never shall my counsels cease to knock
   At thy impatient ears till they fly in   85
   And salve with Christian patience pagan sin.   *Exeunt.*

[IV.ii] *Enter* Vincentio, *with a letter in his hand,* [*and*] Bassiolo.

BASSIOLO.
   This is her letter, sir; you now shall see
   How seely a thing 'tis in respect of mine
   And what a simple woman she has prov'd
   To refuse mine for hers. I pray, look here.
VINCENTIO.
   Soft, sir, I know not, I being her sworn servant,   5
   If I may put up these disgraceful words,
   Given of my mistress, without touch of honor.
BASSIOLO.
   Disgraceful words? I protest I speak not
   To disgrace her, but to grace myself.
VINCENTIO [*accepting Bassiolo's letter*].
   Nay then, sir, if it be to grace yourself,   10

---

  81. *pile*] arrowhead.
[IV.ii]
  2. *seely*] silly.
  2. *in respect of*] in comparison with.
  6. *put up*] put up with (*OED*).
  6. *disgraceful*] disparaging (though *OED* cites this sense only from 1640).
  7. *Given of*] spoken about.
  7. *touch of honor*] taint to my honor.

  I am content; but otherwise, you know,
  I was to take exceptions to a king.

BASSIOLO.

  Nay, y'are i'th' right for that. But read, I pray; if there be
  not more choice words in that letter than in any three of
  Guevara's *Golden Epistles*, I am a very ass. [Vincentio 15
  reads.] How think you, Vince?

VINCENTIO.

  By heaven, no less, sir; it is the best thing—   *He rends it.*
  Gods, what a beast am I!

BASSIOLO [*taking the pieces*]. It is no matter;
  I can set it together again.

VINCENTIO.

  Pardon me, sir; I protest I was ravish'd. But was it possible 20
  she should prefer hers before this?

BASSIOLO.

  O sir, she cried, "Fie upon this."

VINCENTIO.

  Well, I must say nothing: love is blind, you know, and can
  find no fault in his beloved.

BASSIOLO.

  Nay, that's most certain.   25

VINCENTIO.

  Gie't me; I'll have this letter.

BASSIOLO.

  No, good Vince, 'tis not worth it.

VINCENTIO.

  I'll ha't, i'faith. [*He takes back Bassiolo's letter*.] Here's
  enough in it to serve for my letters as long as I live; I'll
  keep it to breed on, as 'twere.   30
  But I much wonder you could make her write.

---

  15. *Guevara's Golden Epistles*] the very popular Spanish work *Epistolas
Familiares* (1539–1545), translated into English by Geoffrey Fenton under
the title *Golden Epistles* (1575). Although somewhat ornate, Fenton's
English style is not similar to Bassiolo's.
  17. S.D.] Vincentio tears the letter, seemingly by accident as he makes
an emphatic movement with it.
  26. *Gie't*] give it.

BASSIOLO.

    Indeed, there were some words belong'd to that.

VINCENTIO.

    How strong an influence works in well-plac'd words,
    And yet there must be a prepared love
    To give those words so mighty a command   35
    Or 'twere impossible they should move so much.
    And will you tell me true?

BASSIOLO.   In anything.

VINCENTIO.

    Does not this lady love you?

BASSIOLO.

    Love me? Why, yes, I think she does not hate me.

VINCENTIO.

    Nay, but i'faith, does she not love you dearly?   40

BASSIOLO.

    No, I protest.

VINCENTIO.   Nor have you never kiss'd her?

BASSIOLO.

    Kiss'd her, that's nothing.

VINCENTIO.   But you know my meaning:
    Have you not been, as one would say, afore me?

BASSIOLO.

    Not I, I swear.

VINCENTIO.   O, y'are too true to tell.

BASSIOLO.

    Nay, by my troth. She has, I must confess,   45
    Us'd me with good respect and nobly still,
    But for such matters—

VINCENTIO [aside].   Very little more
    Would make him take her maidenhead upon him.—
    Well, friend, I rest yet in a little doubt
    This was not hers.   [He points to Margaret's letter.]

BASSIOLO.   'Twas, by that light that shines,   50
    And I'll go fetch her to you to confirm it.

45. by] *Shepherd*; be *Q* .

---

32. *there . . . that*] i.e., it took some doing.
46. *still*] always.

VINCENTIO.

    O, passing friend.

BASSIOLO.

    But when she comes, in any case be bold

    And come upon her with some pleasing thing

    To show y'are pleas'd, however she behaves her;   55

    As, for example, if she turn her back,

    Use you that action you would do before

    And court her thus:

    "Lady, your back part is as fair to me

    As is your forepart."   60

VINCENTIO.

    'Twill be most pleasing.

BASSIOLO.   Ay, for if you love

    One part above another, 'tis a sign

    You like not all alike; and the worst part

    About your mistress you must think as fair,

    As sweet and dainty as the very best,   65

    So much for so much, and considering too

    Each several limb and member in his kind.

VINCENTIO.

    As a man should.

BASSIOLO.   True. Will you think of this?

VINCENTIO.

    I hope I shall.

BASSIOLO.   But if she chance to laugh,

    You must not lose your countenance, but devise   70

    Some speech to show you pleas'd even being laugh'd at.

VINCENTIO.

    Ay, but what speech?

BASSIOLO.

    God's precious, man! Do something of yourself!

    But I'll devise a speech.   *He studies.*

55. pleas'd, . . . her;] *Parrott* (*ess.*);
pleasde: . . . her, *Q* .

---

    52. *passing*] very great.

    54. *come upon . . . thing*] approach . . . saying; but there is a double meaning.

    57.] i.e., do whatever you were going to do.

    67. *in his kind*] according to its nature.

VINCENTIO [*aside*].   Inspire him, Folly.

BASSIOLO.

    Or 'tis no matter: be but bold enough   75
    And laugh when she laughs, and it is enough.
    I'll fetch her to you.   *Exit.*

VINCENTIO.

    Now was there ever such a demilance
    To bear a man so clear through thick and thin?

Enter Bassiolo.

BASSIOLO.

    Or hark you, sir, if she should steal a laughter   80
    Under her fan, thus you may say: "Sweet lady,
    If you will laugh and lie down, I am pleas'd."

VINCENTIO.

    And so I were, by heaven; how know you that?

BASSIOLO.

    'Slid, man, I'll hit your very thoughts in these things.

VINCENTIO.

    Fetch her, sweet friend; I'll hit your words, I warrant.   85

BASSIOLO.

    Be bold then, Vince, and press her to it hard:
    A shamefac'd man is of all women barr'd.   *Exit.*

VINCENTIO.

    How eas'ly worthless men take worth upon them
    And, being overcredulous of their own worths,
    Do underprize as much the worth of others: 90
    The fool is rich, and absurd riches thinks
    All merit is rung out where his purse chinks.

Enter Bassiolo *and* Margaret [, *who coyly turns her back*].

---

78. *demilance*] light horseman, here used contemptuously like "cavalier" (*OED*).

79. *clear*] unharmed.

82. *laugh . . . down*] an obsolete game of cards, often used with double meaning.

84. *'Slid*] by God's eyelid.

85. *hit*] imitate exactly.

91–92. *riches . . . chinks*] riches (personified) thinks there is no merit except that proclaimed (*rung out*) by the chink of his purse.

BASSIOLO.

    My lord, with much entreaty here's my lady.—

    Nay, madam, look not back. —Why, Vince, I say!

MARGARET [aside].

    Vince? O monstrous jest!

BASSIOLO.   To her, for shame.   95

VINCENTIO.

    Lady, your back part is as sweet to me

    As all your forepart.

BASSIOLO [aside].

    He miss'd a little: he said her back part was sweet, when he

    should have said fair. But see, she laughs most fitly to bring

    in the tother.—   100

    [Aside to Vincentio.]   Vince, to her again; she laughs.

VINCENTIO.   Laugh you, fair dame?

    If you will laugh and lie down, I am pleas'd.

MARGARET.

    What villainous stuff is here?

BASSIOLO.

    Sweet mistress, of mere grace enbolden now

    The kind young prince here: it is only love,   105

    Upon my protestation, that thus daunts

    His most heroic spirit. So a while

    I'll leave you close together. —Vince, I say!   *Exit.*

MARGARET.

    O horrible hearing! Does he call you Vince?

VINCENTIO.

    O ay, what else? And I made him embrace me,   110

    Knitting a most familiar league of friendship.

MARGARET.

    But wherefore did you court me so absurdly?

VINCENTIO.

    Gods me, he taught me; I spake out of him.

MARGARET.

    O fie upon't, could you for pity make him

    Such a poor creature? 'Twas abuse enough   115

    99–100. *fitly . . . tother*] conveniently for bringing in the other (speech).

    106. *Upon my protestation*] I swear. Bassiolo thinks Margaret shocked by

Vincentio's seeming reticence, not by the words which Bassiolo inspired.

    108. *close*] privately.

To make him take on him such saucy friendship.
And yet his place is great, for he's not only
My father's usher, but the world's beside,
Because he goes before it all in folly.

VINCENTIO.

    Well, in these homely wiles must our loves mask   120
    Since power denies him his apparent right.

MARGARET.

    But is there no mean to dissolve that power
    And to prevent all further wrong to us
    Which it may work by forcing marriage rites
    Betwixt me and the duke?

VINCENTIO.   No mean but one,   125
    And that is closely to be married first,
    Which I perceive not how we can perform,
    For at my father's coming back from hunting,
    I fear your father and himself resolve
    To bar my interest with his present nuptials.   130

MARGARET.

    That shall they never do. May not we now
    Our contract make and marry before heaven?
    Are not the laws of God and Nature more
    Than formal laws of men? Are outward rites
    More virtuous than the very substance is   135
    Of holy nuptials solemniz'd within?
    Or shall laws made to curb the common world,
    That would not be contain'd in form without them,
    Hurt them that are a law unto themselves?

---

119. *goes before*] Gentlemen ushers led processions.

121. *him*] their love. Parrott suggested reading *love* for *loves* in l. 120.

126. *closely*] secretly. Clandestine marriages were illicit except under very strict conditions, of which parental objection was not one. Oaths such as Vincentio and Margaret are to take were, however, binding whether clandestine or not; the parties could be prevented from marrying each other, but could not be compelled to marry anyone else. See Introduction, p. xv, n. 15.

130. *present*] immediate.

134. *formal laws*] laws governing formalities.

135. *virtuous*] efficacious.

138. *contain'd in form*] kept under control. The contrast between common men and special, superior men is typical of Chapman's thought.

My princely love, 'tis not a priest shall let us,   140
But since th'eternal acts of our pure souls
Knit us with God, the soul of all the world,
He shall be priest to us, and with such rites
As we can here devise we will express
And strongly ratify our hearts' true vows   145
Which no external violence shall dissolve.

VINCENTIO.

This is our only mean t'enjoy each other,
And, my dear life, I will devise a form
To execute the substance of our minds
In honor'd nuptials. First, then, hide your face   150
With this your spotless white and virgin veil;
Now this my scarf I'll knit about your arm
As you shall knit this other end on mine.
And as I knit it, here I vow by heaven;
By the most sweet imaginary joys   155
Of untried nuptials; by love's ushering fire,
Fore-melting beauty, and love's flame itself,
As this is soft and pliant to your arm
In a circumferent flexure, so will I
Be tender of your welfare and your will   160
As of mine own, as of my life and soul,
In all things and forever. Only you
Shall have this care in fullness, only you
Of all dames shall be mine, and only you
I'll court, commend, and joy in till I die.   165

MARGARET.

With like conceit on your arm this I tie
And here, in sight of heaven, by it I swear;
By my love to you, which commands my life;

---

140. *let*] prevent.

150 ff.] Parrott compares the marriage ceremony in *Hero and Leander*, V.352–358.

155. *imaginary*] imagined (since they are as yet *untried*).

156–157. *love's . . . beauty*] beauty, the fire which brings on love, melting all before it. Cf. V.iv.108–109. The conception is Platonic, and the word *ushering* points up the contrast with the sort of ceremony represented by the usher Bassiolo.

159. *circumferent flexure*] circle.

163. *care in fullness*] my exclusive care.

By the dear price of such a constant husband
As you have vowed to be; and by the joy   170
I shall embrace, by all means to requite you:
I'll be as apt to govern as this silk,
As private as my face is to this veil,
And as far from offense as this from blackness.
I will be courted of no man but you;   175
In and for you shall be my joys and woes:
If you be sick, I will be sick though well;
If you be well, I will be well though sick;
Yourself alone my complete world shall be
Even from this hour to all eternity.   180

VINCENTIO.

It is enough, and binds as much as marriage.

Enter Bassiolo.

BASSIOLO [*aside*].

I'll see in what plight my poor lover stands.
Gods me! 'a beckons me to have me gone.
It seems he's enter'd into some good vein.
I'll hence: Love cureth when he vents his pain.   *Exit.* 185

VINCENTIO.

Now, my sweet life, we both remember well,
What we have vow'd shall all be kept entire,
Maugre our fathers' wraths, danger and death.
And to confirm this shall we spend our breath?
Be well advis'd, for yet your choice shall be   190
In all things as before, as large and free.

MARGARET.

What I have vow'd I'll keep even past my death.

---

169. *price*] worth.
172. *apt to govern*] compliant.
173. *private*] exclusive to you.
174. *this*] this white veil.
183. *'a*] he.
184. *vein*] subject of conversation, but there is a double meaning.
185. *vents his pain*] (1) in conversation, (2) through sexual release.
188. *Maugre*] despite.
190–191.] "Consider it well, for your decision shall be as unhampered as before your marriage" (Parrott).

VINCENTIO.

> And I. And now, in token I dissolve
> Your virgin state, I take this snowy veil
> From your much fairer face and claim the dues   195
> Of sacred nuptials. [*They kiss.*] —And now, fairest heaven,
> As thou art infinitely rais'd from earth,
> Diff'rent and opposite, so bless this match,
> As far remov'd from Custom's popular sects
> And as unstain'd with her abhorr'd respects.   200

Enter Bassiolo.

BASSIOLO.

> Mistress, away. Pogio runs up and down
> Calling for Lord Vincentio. Come away,
> For hitherward he bends his clamorous haste.

MARGARET.

> Remember, love.   *Exit* Margaret *and* Bassiolo.

VINCENTIO.   Or else forget me heaven.—

> Why am I sought for by this Pogio?   205
> The ass is great with child of some ill news;
> His mouth is never fill'd with other sound.

Enter Pogio.

POGIO.

> Where is my Lord Vincentio? Where is my lord?

VINCENTIO.

> Here he is, ass. What an exclaiming keep'st thou!

POGIO.

> 'Slud, my lord, I have followed you up and down like a   210
> Tantalus pig till I have worn out my hose hereabouts, I'll

198. Diff'rent] *Q corr*; different *Q uncorr.*

---

193. *in . . . dissolve*] as a symbolic dissolution of.

199. *As far*] i.e., as heaven is above earth.

199. *Custom's popular sects*] "the conventional beliefs of the populace" (Parrott).

211. *Tantalus pig*] Tantony (St. Anthony's) pig; St. Anthony was the patron of swineherds, but Pogio has confused his name with that of the Greek mythological figure. Near St. Anthony's hospital in London many pigs ran loose, and when anyone fed them anything, they would thereafter recognize him and follow him. Hence the phrase "to follow like a Tantony pig" (Parrott).

211. *hose*] breeches. Pogio would not wear out his *hose* by walking.

be sworn, and yet you call me ass still. But I can tell you
passing ill news, my lord.

VINCENTIO.

I know that well, sir; thou never bring'st other. What's your
news now, I pray?   215

POGIO.

O lord, my lord uncle is shot in the side with an arrow.

VINCENTIO.

Plagues take thy tongue! Is he in any danger?

POGIO.

O, danger, ay, he has lien speechless this two hours and
talks so idly.

VINCENTIO.

Accursed news! Where is he? Bring me to him.   220

POGIO.

Yes, do you lead, and I'll guide you to him.   *Exeunt.*

[IV.iii] *Enter* Strozza, *brought in a chair*, Cynanche, *with others.*

CYNANCHE.

How fares it now with my dear lord and husband?

STROZZA.

Come near me, wife; I fare the better far
For the sweet food of thy divine advice.
Let no man value at a little price
A virtuous woman's counsel; her wing'd spirit   5
Is feather'd oftentimes with heavenly words
And, like her beauty, ravishing and pure:
The weaker body, still the stronger soul.
When good endeavors do her powers apply,
Her love draws nearest man's felicity.   10

219. idly] *Shepherd*; idlely *Q* .   "*Cynanche. Benenemus, with*" *Q* .
[IV.iii]   3–4. advice. . . . price] *Shepherd*;
0.1. Cynanche, *with*] *Parrott*;   aduice, . . . price. *Q* .

---

218. *lien*] lain.
[IV.iii]
  8. *still*] ever.
  9. *do . . . apply*] put her powers to use.

O, what a treasure is a virtuous wife,
Discreet and loving. Not one gift on earth
Makes a man's life so highly bound to heaven.
She gives him double forces, to endure
And to enjoy, by being one with him,   15
Feeling his joys and griefs with equal sense;
And, like the twins Hippocrates reports,
If he fetch sighs, she draws her breath as short;
If he lament, she melts herself in tears;
If he be glad, she triumphs; if he stir,   20
She moves his way, in all things his sweet ape,
And is in alterations passing strange,
Himself divinely varied without change.
Gold is right precious, but his price infects
With pride and avarice. Authority lifts   25
Hats from men's heads and bows the strongest knees,
Yet cannot bend in rule the weakest hearts.
Music delights but one sense, nor choice meats:
One quickly fades, the other stir to sin.
But a true wife both sense and soul delights   30
And mixeth not her good with any ill;
Her virtues, ruling hearts, all pow'rs command;
All store, without her, leaves a man but poor,
And with her, poverty is exceeding store;
No time is tedious with her; her true worth   35
Makes a true husband think his arms enfold,
With her alone, a complete world of gold.

22. alterations] *Shepherd*; alteratious   29. stir] *Q* (stirre); stirs *Parrott*.
Q.

---

17. *twins . . . reports*] Hippocrates, the "father of medicine," is said to have
"pronounced a pair of brothers twins from the fact that both sickened at the
same time and that the progress of the disease was similar and simultaneous
in both cases" (Parrott).

20. *triumphs*] rejoices.

22–23.] she is very reluctant to be different from him; she assumes his
identity, divinely varied (as Eve was made different from Adam) but
without essential difference.

24. *his*] its.

27. *bend in rule*] bend into submission.

28. *nor choice meats*] nor are choice meats sufficiently pleasurable.

33. *store*] abundance.

CYNANCHE.

    I wish, dear love, I could deserve as much
    As your most kind conceit hath well express'd;
    But when my best is done, I see you wounded   40
    And neither can recure nor ease your pains.

STROZZA.

    Cynanche, thy advice hath made me well:
    My free submission to the hand of heaven
    Makes it redeem me from the rage of pain.
    For though I know the malice of my wound   45
    Shoots still the same distemper through my veins,
    Yet the judicial patience I embrace,
    In which my mind spreads her impassive pow'rs
    Through all my suff'ring parts, expels their frailty
    And, rendering up their whole life to my soul,   50
    Leaves me nought else but soul, and so like her,
    Free from the passions of my fuming blood.

CYNANCHE.

    Would God you were so, and that too much pain
    Were not the reason you felt sense of none.

STROZZA.

    Think'st thou me mad, Cynanche? For madmen,   55
    By pains ungovern'd, have no sense of pain.
    But I, I tell you, am quite contrary,
    Eas'd with well governing my submitted pain.
    Be cheer'd then, wife, and look not for, in me,
    The manners of a common wounded man.   60
    Humility hath rais'd me to the stars,
    In which, as in a sort of crystal globes,
    I sit and see things hid from human sight;
    Ay, even the very accidents to come

---

41. *recure*] cure.

47. *judicial*] judicious.

48. *impassive*] incapable of feeling pain (though *OED* cites it only from 1667). The patient mind passes on this power to the body.

52. *fuming*] raging.

58. *submitted*] brought under my control.

62. *crystal globes*] crystal balls; the conception is probably also related to the old idea of the universe as a set of concentric transparent spheres in which the planets and the stars traveled about the earth.

64. *accidents*] unforeseen events.

Are present with my knowledge. The seventh day   65
The arrowhead will fall out of my side;
The seventh day, wife, the forked head will out.

CYNANCHE.

Would God it would, my lord, and leave you well.

STROZZA.

Yes, the seventh day I am assur'd it will,
And I shall live, I know it; I thank heaven,   70
I know it well. And I'll teach my physician
To build his cares hereafter upon heaven
More than on earthly med'cines, for I know
Many things shown me from the open'd skies
That pass all arts. Now my physician   75
Is coming to me; he makes friendly haste,
And I will well requite his care of me.

CYNANCHE.

How know you he is coming?

STROZZA.   Passing well,
And that my dear friend Lord Vincentio
Will presently come see me too. I'll stay   80
My good physician till my true friend come.

CYNANCHE [aside].

Ay me, his talk is idle and, I fear,
Foretells his reasonable soul now leaves him.

STROZZA.

Bring my physician in; he's at the door.

CYNANCHE.

Alas, there's no physician.

STROZZA.   But I know it.   85
See, he is come.

Enter Benevenius.

BENEVENIUS.   How fares my worthy lord?

81. My physician] *Shepherd; in par-*   86. S.D. Benevenius] *Yamada;*
entheses in Q.   "*Beneuemius*" *Q.*

72. *cares*] If not a mistake for "cures" (as Parrott persuasively states), it is simply the plural of the word used in "doctor's care."

75. *pass all arts*] surpass all human knowledge.

80. *stay*] detain.

83. *reasonable soul*] the reasoning part of Strozza's soul; she fears that his seeming irrationality signals his impending death.

STROZZA.

    Good doctor, I endure no pain at all,

    And the seventh day the arrow's head will out.

BENEVENIUS.

    Why should it fall out the seventh day, my lord?

STROZZA.

    I know it; the seventh day it will not fail.   90

BENEVENIUS.

    I wish it may, my lord.

STROZZA.   Yes, 'twill be so.

    You come with purpose to take present leave,

    But you shall stay a while; my Lord Vincentio

    Would see you fain and now is coming hither.

BENEVENIUS.

    How knows your lordship? Have you sent for him?   95

STROZZA.

    No, but 'tis very true; he's now hard by

    And will not hinder your affairs a whit.

BENEVENIUS [*aside*].

    How want of rest distempers his light brain!—

    Brings my lord any train?

STROZZA.   None but himself;

    My nephew Pogio now hath left his grace.   100

    Good doctor, go and bring him by his hand,

    Which he will give you, to my longing eyes.

BENEVENIUS.

    'Tis strange if this be true.   *Exit.*

CYNANCHE.   The prince, I think,

    Yet knows not of your hurt.

Enter Vincentio *holding the Doctor's hand.*

STROZZA.   Yes, wife, too well.

    See, he is come. —Welcome, my princely friend.   105

    I have been shot, my lord, but the seventh day

    The arrow's head will fall out of my side,

    And I shall live.

VINCENTIO.   I do not fear your life.—

    But doctor, is it your opinion

    That the seventh day the arrowhead will out?   110

98. *light*] delirious.

STROZZA.

    No, 'tis not his opinion; 'tis my knowledge,
    For I do know it well. And I do wish,
    Even for your only sake, my noble lord,
    This were the seventh day and I now were well,
    That I might be some strength to your hard state,   115
    For you have many perils to endure:
    Great is your danger, great; your unjust ill
    Is passing foul and mortal. Would to God
    My wound were something well, I might be with you.—
                      [Cynanche *and* Benevenius *whisper.*]
    Nay, do not whisper; I know what I say—   120
    Too well for you, my lord. I wonder heaven
    Will let such violence threat an innocent life.

VINCENTIO.

    What'er it be, dear friend, so you be well,
    I will endure it all; your wounded state
    Is all the danger I fear towards me.   125

STROZZA.

    Nay, mine is nothing, for the seventh day
    This arrowhead will out and I shall live.
    And so shall you, I think, but very hardly;
    It will be hardly you will 'scape indeed.

VINCENTIO.

    Be as will be. Pray heaven your prophecy   130
    Be happily accomplished in yourself,
    And nothing then can come amiss to me.

STROZZA.

    What says my doctor? Thinks he I say true?

BENEVENIUS.

    If your good lordship could but rest a while,
    I would hope well.

STROZZA.   Yes, I shall rest, I know,   135
    If that will help your judgment.

BENEVENIUS.   Yes, it will,
    And good my lord, let's help you in to try.

STROZZA.

    You please me much; I shall sleep instantly.   *Exeunt.*

---

119. *something*] somewhat.

[IV.iv]   *Enter* Alphonso *and* Medice.

ALPHONSO.

    Why should the humorous boy forsake the chase

    As if he took advantage of my absence

    To some act that my presence would offend?

MEDICE.

    I warrant you, my lord, 'tis to that end,

    And I believe he wrongs you in your love.   5

    Children, presuming on their parents' kindness,

    Care not what unkind actions they commit

    Against their quiet. And were I as you,

    I would affright my son from these bold parts

    And father him as I found his deserts.   10

ALPHONSO.

    I swear I will; and, can I prove he aims

    At any interruption in my love,

    I'll interrupt his life.

MEDICE.   We soon shall see,

    For I have made Madam Corteza search

    With picklocks all the ladies' cabinets   15

    About Earl Lasso's house, and if there be

    Traffic of love 'twixt any one of them

    And your suspected son, 'twill soon appear

    In some sign of their amorous merchandise.

    See where she comes, loaded with gems and papers.   20

Enter Corteza.

CORTEZA.

    See here, my lord, I have robb'd all their caskets.

    Know you this ring? this carcanet? this chain?

    Will any of these letters serve your turn?

ALPHONSO.

    I know not these things, but come, let me read

    Some of these letters.   [*He reads.*]

---

1. *humorous*] capricious.
3. *offend*] prevent.
9. *parts*] acts.
10. *father*] be such a father to.
19. *merchandise*] exchanges.
22. *carcanet*] necklace.

MEDICE.   Madam, in this deed   25
   You deserve highly of my lord the duke.
CORTEZA.
   Nay, my Lord Medice, I think I told you
   I could do pretty well in these affairs.
   O, these young girls engross up all the love
   From us poor beldames, but I hold my hand;   30
   I'll ferret all the cunni-holes of their kindness
   Ere I have done with them.
ALPHONSO.   Passion of death!
   See, see, Lord Medice, my trait'rous son
   Hath long joy'd in the favors of my love.—
                      [Medice *takes a letter and reads it.*]
   Woe to the womb that bore him, and my care   35
   To bring him up to this accursed hour
   In which all cares possess my wretched life.
MEDICE.
   What father would believe he had a son
   So full of treachery to his innocent state?
   And yet, my lord, this letter shows no meeting,   40
   But a desire to meet.
CORTEZA.   Yes, yes, my lord,
   I do suspect they meet, and I believe
   I know well where, too; I believe I do.
   And therefore tell me, does no creature know
   That you have left the chase thus suddenly   45
   And are come hither? Have you not been seen
   By any of these lovers?
ALPHONSO.   Not by any.

25. S.P. MEDICE] *Parrott*; *"Lass." Q* .

---

   29. *engross up*] absorb.
   30. *beldames*] matrons (but with unintentional connotations of the virago).
   31. *cunni-holes*] The old spelling suggests the pun: (1) coney-holes (rabbit-holes), (2) vaginas.
   31. *kindness*] affections.
   46–47. *Have . . . lovers?*] The question recalls Strozza's promise to warn Vincentio of Alphonso's return (III.ii.297); subplot and main plot are subtly linked because Strozza's wound prevented him from keeping his promise.

CORTEZA.

    Come then, come follow me; I am persuaded
    I shall go near to show you their kind hands.
    Their confidence that you are still a-hunting   50
    Will make your amorous son that stole from thence
    Bold in his love-sports. Come, come, a fresh chase:
    I hold this picklock; you shall hunt at view.
    What, do they think to 'scape? An old wife's eye
    Is a blue crystal full of sorcery.   55

ALPHONSO.

    If this be true, the trait'rous boy shall die.   *Exeunt.*

[IV.v]   *Enter* Lasso [*and*] Margaret, Bassiolo *going before.*

LASSO.

    Tell me, I pray you, what strange hopes they are
    That feed your coy conceits against the duke
    And are preferr'd before th'assured greatness
    His highness graciously would make your fortunes.

MARGARET.

    I have small hopes, my lord, but a desire   5
    To make my nuptial choice of one I love;
    And, as I would be loath t'impair my state,
    So I affect not honors that exceed it.

LASSO.

    O, you are very temp'rate in your choice,
    Pleading a judgment past your sex and years,   10
    But I believe some fancy will be found

54. wife's] *Shepherd*; wiues *Q*.   *Parrott.*
IV.v.] *Yamada*; *no new scene in*

---

49. *go . . . hands*] be on the point of showing you their affectionate hands.

52. *fresh chase*] a new quarry (to be hunted).

53. *hunt at view*] hunt with the quarry in sight (not merely by scent).

54. *old wife*] old woman, traditionally associated with fantastic stories especially of supernatural occurrences and here with supernatural knowledge, as from a *crystal* ball.

[IV.v]

7. *impair my state*] lower my station (by marrying beneath her rank).

11. *fancy*] (1) amorous inclination toward someone, (2) fantasy (as distinct from *judgment*, l. 10).

The forge of these gay glozes. If it be,
I shall decipher what close traitor 'tis
That is your agent in your secret plots—

BASSIOLO [*aside*].
  'Swounds!   15

LASSO.
  And him for whom you plot; and on you all
I will revenge thy disobedience
With such severe correction as shall fright
All such deluders from the like attempts;
But chiefly he shall smart that is your factor.   20

BASSIOLO [*aside*].
  O me accurs'd!

LASSO.   Meantime I'll cut
Your poor craft short, i'faith.

MARGARET.   Poor craft indeed
That I or any others use for me.

LASSO.
  Well, dame, if it be nothing but the jar
Of your unfitted fancy that procures   25
Your wilful coyness to my lord the duke,
No doubt but time and judgment will conform it
To such obedience as so great desert,
Propos'd to your acceptance, doth require—
To which end do you counsel her, Bassiolo—   30
And let me see, maid, 'gainst the duke's return,
Another tincture set upon your looks
Than heretofore. For be assur'd, at last
Thou shalt consent or else incur my curse.—
Advise her you, Bassiolo.   *Exit.*

BASSIOLO.   Ay, my good lord.—   35
God's pity, what an errant ass was I

---

12. *forge . . . glozes*] smithy (source) of these specious deceits.
13. *close*] secret.
20. *factor*] agent.
22. *craft . . . craft*] slyness . . . power, art.
24. *jar*] discord.
25. *unfitted*] not provided with something suitable, like reason (*OED*, citing this line).
31. *'gainst*] in preparation for.

To entertain the prince's crafty friendship!
'Slud, I half suspect the villain gull'd me!

MARGARET.

Our squire, I think, is startl'd.

BASSIOLO.   Nay, lady, it is true,
And you must frame your fancy to the duke,   40
For I protest I will not be corrupted
For all the friends and fortunes in the world
To gull my lord that trusts me.

MARGARET.   O sir, now,
Y'are true too late.

BASSIOLO.   No, lady, not a whit.
'Slud, and you think to make an ass of me,   45
May chance to rise betimes; I know't, I know.

MARGARET.

Out, servile coward. Shall a light suspect
That hath no slend'rest proof of what we do
Infringe the weighty faith that thou hast sworn
To thy dear friend the prince, that dotes on thee   50
And will in pieces cut thee for thy falsehood?

BASSIOLO.

I care not; I'll not hazard my estate
For any prince on earth, and I'll disclose
The complot to your father if you yield not
To his obedience.

MARGARET.   Do if thou dar'st,   55
Even for thy scrap'd-up living and thy life.
I'll tell my father then how thou didst woo me
To love the young prince and didst force me, too,
To take his letters; I was well inclin'd,
I will be sworn, before, to love the duke,   60
But thy vile railing at him made me hate him.

BASSIOLO.

I rail at him?

MARGARET.   Ay, marry, did you, sir,
And said he was a pattern for a potter

45–46. *and . . . betimes*] "If you mean to make an ass of me, you must get up early" (Parrott).
47. *light suspect*] slight suspicion.
54. *complot*] conspiracy.

  Fit t'have his picture stamp'd on a stone jug
  To keep ale-knights in memory of sobriety.   65
BASSIOLO [*aside*].

  Sh'as a plaguey memory.
MARGARET.

  I could have lov'd him else—nay, I did love him,
  Though I dissembled it to bring him on,
  And I by this time might have been a duchess.
  And, now I think on't better, for revenge   70
  I'll have the duke, and he shall have thy head
  For thy false wit within it to his love.
  Now go and tell my father; pray be gone.
BASSIOLO.

  Why, and I will go.
MARGARET.   Go, for God's sake go.

  Are you here yet?
BASSIOLO.   Well, now I am resolv'd. [*He starts to go.*] 75
MARGARET.

  'Tis bravely done; farewell. But do you hear, sir?
  Take this with you besides: the young prince keeps
  A certain letter you had writ for me—
  "Endearing" and "condoling" and "mature"—
  And if you should deny things, that, I hope,   80
  Will stop your impudent mouth. But go your ways;
  If you can answer all this, why 'tis well.
BASSIOLO [*coming back*].

  Well, lady, if you will assure me here
  You will refrain to meet with the young prince,
  I will say nothing.
MARGARET.   Good sir, say your worst, 85
  For I will meet him, and that presently.
BASSIOLO.

  Then be content, I pray, and leave me out,
  And meet hereafter as you can yourselves.
MARGARET.

  No, no, sir, no, 'tis you must fetch him to me,
  And you shall fetch him, or I'll do your errand. 90

---

90. errand] *Q corr.* (arrand);   errant *Q uncorr.*

 90. *I'll . . . errand*] i.e., I'll tell my father.

BASSIOLO [*aside*].

> 'Swounds, what a spite is this! I will resolve
> T'endure the worst; 'tis but my foolish fear
> The plot will be discover'd. —O the gods!
> 'Tis the best sport to play with these young dames.
> I have dissembl'd, mistress, all this while.   95
> Have I not made you in a pretty taking?

MARGARET.

> O, 'tis most good; thus you may play on me.
> You cannot be content to make me love
> A man I hated till you spake for him
> With such enchanting speeches as no friend   100
> Could possibly resist, but you must use
> Your villainous wit to drive me from my wits.
> A plague of that bewitching tongue of yours!
> Would I had never heard your scurvy words.

BASSIOLO.

> Pardon, dear dame, I'll make amends, i'faith.   105
> Think you that I'll play false with my dear Vince?
> I swore that sooner Hybla should want bees
> And Italy bona-robas than I faith,
> And so they shall.
> Come, you shall meet and double meet, in spite   110
> Of all your foes and dukes that dare maintain them.
> A plague of all old doters; I disdain them.

MARGARET.

> Said like a friend.   [*Aside*.]   O, let me comb the cockscomb.
>
> *Exeunt.*

Finis Actus Quarti.

93. gods!] *Q corr.*; gods, *Q uncorr.*   113. the] *Q* ; thy *Parrott, who does not*
108. I] *Parrott*; I; *Q corr.*; I, *Q*   *read as an aside.*
uncorr.

---

96. *made . . . taking*] put you into a fine state.

112. *doters*] (1) lovers, (2) dotards.

113. *let . . . cockscomb*] essentially, o what a fool! (the cockscomb being a
fool's hat). The literal sense of the words is unclear; perhaps Margaret is
running her fingers through Bassiolo's hair in apparent affection.

[V.i]   *Enter* Alphonso, Medice, Lasso, [*and*] Corteza *above*.

CORTEZA.

> Here is the place will do the deed, i'faith;
> This, duke, will show thee how youth puts down age,
> Ay, and perhaps how youth does put down youth.

ALPHONSO.

> If I shall see my love in any sort
> Prevented or abus'd, th'abuser dies.   5

LASSO.

> I hope there is no such intent, my liege,
> For sad as death should I be to behold it.

MEDICE.

> You must not be too confident, my lord,
> Or in your daughter or in them that guard her.
> The prince is politic and envies his father,   10
> And, though not for himself nor any good
> Intended to your daughter, yet because
> He knows 'twould kill his father, he would seek her.

CORTEZA.

> Whist, whist; they come.

>   *Enter* Bassiolo, Vincentio, *and* Margaret [*below*].

BASSIOLO.   Come, meet me boldly, come,

> And let them come from hunting when they dare.   15

VINCENTIO.

> H'as the best spirit.

BASSIOLO.   Spirit? What a plague!

> Shall a man fear capriches? —[*To* Margaret.]   You,
>   forsooth,

0.1. *above*] on the upper stage, or gallery, But Smith (p. 393) placed them in a side gallery (see note to l. 14. S.D.).

2–3. *puts down . . . put down*] overcomes . . . lay down (for sexual intercourse).

9. *Or . . . or*] either . . . or.

14. S.D. *below*] on the main stage. From now through l. 125 the characters above can see and hear Bassiolo, Vincentio, and Margaret, but are neither seen nor heard by them. Smith (p. 393) placed the lovers in an inner stage.

17. *capriches*] caprices (an earlier use than any cited in *OED*).

Must have your love come t'ye, and when he comes,
Then you grow shamefac'd and he must not touch you,
But "Fie, my father comes!" and "Faugh, my aunt!"   20
O, 'tis a witty hearing, is't not, think you?

VINCENTIO.

Nay, pray thee do not mock her, gentle friend.

BASSIOLO.

Nay, you are even as wise a wooer too:
If she turn from you, you even let her turn
And say you do not love to force a lady,   25
'Tis too much rudeness. Gosh hat, what's a lady?
Must she not be touch'd? What, is she copper, think you,
And will not bide the touchstone? Kiss her, Vince,
And thou dost love me, kiss her.

VINCENTIO.   Lady, now
I were too simple if I should not offer.   30

                              [*He offers to kiss her.*]

MARGARET.

O God, sir, pray, away; this man talks idly.

BASSIOLO.

How shay by that? Now by that candle there,
Were I as Vince is, I would handle you
In rufty-tufty wise, in your right kind.

MARGARET [*aside to* Vincentio].

O, you have made him a sweet beagle, ha'y' not?   35

VINCENTIO [*aside to* Margaret].

'Tis the most true believer in himself
Of all that sect of Folly; faith's his fault.

---

31. idly] *Shepherd*; idlely *Q*.   *corr.*; himself, *Q uncorr.*
36. 'Tis] *Shepherd*; T'is *Q corr.*; T's   37. Folly;] *Q uncorr.* (follie); follie
Q uncorr.   *Q corr.*
36. himself] *Parrott*; himselfe: *Q*

---

26. *Gosh hat*] presumably God's heart (Parrott) or God save it. Bassiolo appears to be drunk (Parrott).

28. *touchstone*] a smooth piece of quartz or jasper used to test the purity of gold, or the amount of gold in a gold-copper alloy, by the mark left on the touchstone.

32. *How shay*] presumably "how say ye?"

34. *rufty-tufty . . . kind*] rudely and roughly, according to your proper nature.

35. *beagle*] loudmouth, from the loud baying of beagle hounds.

BASSIOLO.

So, to her, Vince; I give thee leave, my lad.
     Sweet were the words my mistress spake
          When tears fell from her eyes.   40

                              He lies down by them.

Thus, as the lion lies before his den
Guarding his whelps and streaks his careless limbs,
And when the panther, fox, or wolf comes near,
He never deigns to rise to fright them hence,
But only puts forth one of his stern paws   45
And keeps his dear whelps safe as in a hutch,
So I present his person and keep mine:
Foxes, go by; I put my terror forth.
          (*Cantat.*) Let all the world say what they can;
               Her bargain best she makes   50
          That hath the wit to choose a man
               To pay for that he takes.
          Belle piu, &c.   *Iterum cantat.*
Dispatch, sweet whelps; the bug, the duke, comes straight.
O, 'tis a grave old lover, that same duke,   55
And chooses minions rarely, if you mark him:
The noble Medice, that man, that Bobbadilla,
That foolish knave, that hose-and-doublet stinkard.

40.1. *He . . . them*] Q *corr.*; *not in*   53. *Belle piu, &c.*] *Parrott*; *apparently*
Q *uncorr.*   *part of S.D. in Q.*
48. *Foxes,*] Q *corr.*; *Foxes* Q *uncorr.*

---

42. *streaks*] strokes.   42. *careless*] carefree.
47. *present*] represent.
48. *Foxes, go by*] "stock phrase to imply impatience of anything disagree-
able, inconvenient, or old-fashioned" (F. S. Boas, ed., *Works of Thomas
Kyd* [Oxford, 1901], p. 405); the phrase is based on Thomas Kyd's *Spanish
Tragedy*, III.xii.31; *go by* means "slink off." Here the lion is imagined as
scorning the animals which *come near*.
49. S.D. *Cantat*] He sings. The song is otherwise unknown.
53. *Belle piu*] "Beauties more"; apparently a refrain of the song.
53. S.D. *Iterum cantat*] He sings it again.
57. *Bobbadilla*] the cowardly braggart in the original version of Ben
Jonson's *Every Man in his Humor*, (printed in Quarto in 1601). Jonson changed
the name to Bobadill in his revision of the play (printed in the 1616 Folio
edition of his *Works*).
58. *hose-and-doublet stinkard*] The phrase suggests lowness of birth, for
one who went in hose and doublet only was without the gown or coat
usually worn by dignity (*OED*, s.v. "Doublet"); cf. I.i.115.

MEDICE.
> 'Swounds, my lord, rise; let's endure no more.

ALPHONSO.
> A little, pray my lord, for I believe   60
> We shall discover very notable knavery.

LASSO.
> Alas, how I am griev'd and sham'd in this.

CORTEZA.
> Never care you, lord brother; there's no harm done.

BASSIOLO.
> But that sweet creature, my good lord's sister,
> Madam Corteza, she, the noblest dame   65
> That ever any vein of honor bled,
> There were a wife, now, for my lord the duke
> Had he the grace to choose her. But indeed,
> To speak her true praise I must use some study.

CORTEZA.
> Now truly, brother, I did ever think   70
> This man the honestest man that e'er you kept.

LASSO.
> So, sister, so, because he praises you.

CORTEZA.
> Nay, sir, but you shall hear him further yet.

BASSIOLO.
> Were not her head sometimes a little light
> And so unapt for matter of much weight,   75
> She were the fittest and the worthiest dame
> To leap a window and to break her neck
> That ever was.

CORTEZA.   God's pity, arrant knave!
> I ever thought him a dissembling varlet.

BASSIOLO [*rising*].
> Well, now, my hearts, be wary, for by this   80
> I fear the duke is coming. I'll go watch
> And give you warning. I commend me t'ye.   *Exit.*

71. honestest] *Q corr.*; honest *Q
uncorr.*

66. *vein . . . bled*] noble line produced.
80. *hearts*] with a pun on *harts*, deer (commonly quarry).
80. *by this*] by this time.

VINCENTIO.

    O, fine phrase.

MARGARET.   And very timely us'd.

VINCENTIO.

    What now, sweet life, shall we resolve upon?

    We never shall enjoy each other here.   85

MARGARET.

    Direct you then, my lord, what we shall do,

    For I am at your will, and will endure

    With you the cruel'st absence from the state

    We both were born to that can be suppos'd.

VINCENTIO.

    That would extremely grieve me: could myself   90

    Only endure the ill our hardest fates

    May lay on both of us, I would not care,

    But to behold thy sufferance, I should die.

MARGARET.

    How can your lordship wrong my love so much

    To think the more woe I sustain for you   95

    Breeds not the more my comfort? I, alas,

    Have no mean else to make my merit even

    In any measure with your eminent worth.

Enter Bassiolo.

BASSIOLO [*aside*].

    Now must I exercise my timorous lovers,

    Like fresh-arm'd soldiers, with some false alarms   100

    To make them yare and wary of their foe,

    The boist'rous bearded duke. I'll rush upon them

    With a most hideous cry. —[*Shouts.*]   The duke, the duke,

      the duke!

                 [Vincentio *and* Margaret *start to flee.*]

    Ha-ha-ha. Wo-ho; come again, I say;

    The duke's not come, i'faith.

VINCENTIO [*returning with* Margaret.] God's precious, man!   105

    What did you mean to put us in this fear?

---

93. *sufferance*] suffering.

100. *fresh-arm'd*] green, untried.

101. *yare*] alert.

104. *Wo-ho*] "the cry used by falconers to recall a hawk" (Parrott).

BASSIOLO.

    O sir, to make you look about the more;

    Nay, we must teach you more of this, I tell you.

    What, can you be too safe, sir? What, I say,

    Must you be pamper'd in your vanities?   110

    [*Aside.*]   Ah, I do domineer and rule the roast.   *Exit.*

MARGARET.

    Was ever such an ingle? Would to God,

    If 'twere not for ourselves, my father saw him.

LASSO.

    Minion, you have your prayer, and my curse,

    For your good housewifery.

MEDICE.   What says your highness?   115

    Can you endure these injuries any more?

ALPHONSO.

    No more, no more; advise me what is best

    To be the penance of my graceless son.

MEDICE.

    My lord, no mean but death or banishment

    Can be fit penance for him if you mean   120

    T'enjoy the pleasure of your love yourself.

CORTEZA.

    Give him plain death, my lord, and then y'are sure.

ALPHONSO.

    Death or his banishment he shall endure

    For wreak of that joy's exile I sustain.

    Come, call our guard and apprehend him straight.   125

              Exeunt [Alphonso, Medice, Lasso, *and* Corteza].

VINCENTIO.

    I have some jewels, then, my dearest life,

    Which, with whatever we can get beside,

    Shall be our means, and we will make escape.

Enter Bassiolo *running.*

---

112. *ingle*] literally, (1) fire, (2) a catamite; here, merely a pejorative epithet.

115. *housewifery*] quality of being a housewife (here ironically, like the derivative word "hussy").

124. *For . . . exile*] in punishment for the loss of joy which.

127. *beside*] besides.

BASSIOLO.

    'Sblood, the duke and all come now in earnest;
    The duke, by heaven, the duke!

VINCENTIO.   Nay then, i'faith   130
    Your jest is too, too stale.

BASSIOLO.   God's precious!
    By these ten bones and by this hat and heart,
    The duke and all comes. See, we are cast away.   *Exeunt.*

[*Before they get off,*] *enter* Alphonso, Medice, Lasso, Corteza, *and* Julio.

ALPHONSO.

    Lay hands upon them all. Pursue, pursue.

LASSO.

    Stay, thou ungracious girl.

              [*He seizes* Margaret; Bassiolo *and* Vincentio *escape.*]

ALPHONSO.   Lord Medice,   135
    Lead you our guard and see you apprehend
    The treacherous boy, nor let him 'scape with life
    Unless he yield to his eternal exile.

MEDICE.

    'Tis princely said, my lord.   *Exit.*

LASSO.   And take my usher.

MARGARET.

    Let me go into exile with my lord;   140
    I will not live if I be left behind.

LASSO.

    Impudent damsel, wouldst thou follow him?

MARGARET.

    He is my husband. Whom else should I follow?

LASSO.

    Wretch, thou speakest treason to my lord, the duke.

138. eternal] *Shepherd*; externall *Q*.
140. exile . . . lord;] *Q corr.* (Lord,);
exile, . . . Lord *Q uncorr.*

    132. *ten bones*] fingers.
    133. S.D. *Exeunt*] As often, the stage direction marks the point at which the characters begin their exits, not that at which they make it through a door.
    139. *take*] capture.

ALPHONSO.

    Yet love me, lady, and I pardon all.   145

MARGARET.

    I have a husband and must love none else.

ALPHONSO.

    Despiteful dame, I'll disinherit him,

    And thy good father here shall cast off thee,

    And both shall feed on air, or starve and die.

MARGARET.

    If this be justice, let it be our dooms;   150

    If free and spotless love in equal years,

    With honors unimpaired, deserve such ends,

    Let us approve what justice is in friends.

LASSO.

    You shall, I swear. —Sister, take you her close

    Into your chamber; lock her fast alone,   155

    And let her stir nor speak with anyone.

CORTEZA.

    She shall not, brother. —Come, niece, come with me.

MARGARET.

    Heaven save my love, and I will suffer gladly.

                   Exeunt Corteza [*and*] Margaret.

ALPHONSO.

    Haste, Julio, follow thou my son's pursuit

    And will Lord Medice not to hurt nor touch him,   160

    But either banish him or bring him back;

    Charge him to use no violence to his life.

JULIO.

    I will, my lord.   *Exit* Julio.

ALPHONSO.   O Nature! how, alas,

    Art thou and Reason, thy true guide, oppos'd!

    More bane thou tak'st to guide Sense led amiss   165

    Than, being guided, Reason gives thee bliss.   *Exeunt.*

149. starve] *Q   uncorr.*   (starue);
starue, *Q   corr.*

---

  153. *approve*] demonstrate.   160. *will*] direct.
  165–166.] You (Nature, here parental nature) receive more pain from correcting the senses (here Vincentio's senses, as opposed to his reason) which have been led astray than you receive pleasure from the due submission of the senses to the reason. To *take one's bane* usually meant to catch one's death.

[V.ii]

Enter Cynanche, Benevenius, *ancilla,* [*and*] Strozza *having the arrowhead.*

STROZZA.

    Now see, good doctor, 'twas no frantic fancy
    That made my tongue presage this head should fall
    Out of my wounded side the seventh day,
    But an inspired rapture of my mind,
    Submitted and conjoin'd in patience   5
    To my creator, in whom I foresaw,
    Like to an angel, this divine event.

BENEVENIUS.

    So is it plain and happily approv'd
    In a right Christian precedent, confirming
    What a most sacred med'cine patience is   10
    That, with the high thirst of our souls' clear fire,
    Exhausts corporeal humor and all pain,
    Casting our flesh off while we it retain.

CYNANCHE.

    Make some religious vow, then, my dear lord,
    And keep it in the proper memory   15
    Of so celestial and free a grace.

STROZZA.

    Sweet wife, thou restest my good angel still,
    Suggesting by all means these ghostly counsels.
    Thou weariest not thy husband's patient ears

10. med'cine] *Q corr.* (medcine);
Medicine *Q uncorr.*

   0.1. *ancilla*] maid.
   0.1. *having*] holding in his hand.
   8. *approv'd*] demonstrated.
   11–13.] United with the Christian dualism of soul and body is the ancient dualism of natural heat, the fire of life (soul); and radical moisture or humor (associated with the body), the fuel of the flame of life. The loss of *corporeal humor* would normally result in the loss of the soul's *clear fire,* i.e., in death. But Benevenius is describing a mysterious Neo-Platonic *rapture* (l. 4) in which patience allows Strozza to transcend his fleshly pain even as he retains his flesh.
   16. *free*] freely given.
   17. *restest*] remain.
   18. *ghostly*] spiritual.

With motions for new fashions in attire,   20
For change of jewels, pastimes, and nice cates;
Nor studiest eminence and the higher place
Amongst thy consorts, like all other dames;
But, knowing more worthy objects appertain
To every woman that desires t'enjoy   25
A blessed life in marriage, thou contemn'st
Those common pleasures and pursu'st the rare,
Using thy husband in those virtuous gifts
For which thou first didst choose him, and thereby
Cloy'st not with him, but lov'st him endlessly.   30
In reverence of thy motion, then, and zeal
To that most sovereign power that was my cure,
I make a vow to go on foot to Rome
And offer humbly in St. Peter's temple
This fatal arrowhead, which work let none judge   35
A superstitious rite, but a right use
Proper to this peculiar instrument
Which, visibly resign'd to memory
Through every eye that sees, will stir the soul
To gratitude and progress in the use   40
Of my tried patience, which, in my powers ending,
Would shut th'example out of future lives.
No act is superstitious that applies
All power to God, devoting hearts through eyes.

---

27. pursu'st] *Q corr.*; pursuest *Q*
uncorr.
28. gifts] *Q uncorr.* (guifts); gifts:
Q corr.
30. lov'st] *Q corr.* (lou'st); louest
Q uncorr.

32. cure,] *Q uncorr.*; cure. *Q corr.*
43–44. No . . . eyes] *three copies of*
Q corr. mark the couplet with quotation
marks.

---

21. *nice cates*] choice foods.
23. *consorts*] companions.
30. *Cloy'st not*] do not grow tired of.
38. *resign'd*] revealed. The process here described is orthodox Renaissance psychophysics: the external senses transmitted impressions to the common sense, which assembled them into composite images and interpreted them; they were then transmitted to the imagination and/or the memory. The passions were then aroused according to whether the imagination found the objects perceived pleasing or painful. See Lawrence Babb, *The Elizabethan Malady* (East Lansing, 1951), pp. 3–4.
41. *in . . . ending*] if it should die with me.

BENEVENIUS.

    Spoke with the true tongue of a nobleman.   45

    But now are all these excitations toys,

    And Honor fats his brain with other joys.

    I know your true friend Prince Vincentio

    Will triumph in this excellent effect

    Of your late prophecy.

STROZZA.   O, my dear friend's name   50

    Presents my thoughts with a most mortal danger

    To his right innocent life: a monstrous fact

    Is now effected on him.

CYNANCHE.   Where? or how?

STROZZA.

    I do not well those circumstances know,

    But am assur'd the substance is too true.   55

    Come, reverend doctor, let us harken out

    Where the young prince remains, and bear with you

    Med'cines t'allay his danger: if by wounds,

    Bear precious balsam or some sovereign juice;

    If by fell poison, some choice antidote;   60

    If by black witchcraft, our good spirits and prayers

    Shall exorcise the devilish wrath of hell

    Out of his princely bosom.

Enter Pogio *running.*

POGIO [*breathlessly*].

    Where—where—where—where's my lord uncle, my lord

    my uncle?   65

STROZZA.

    Here's the ill-tidings-bringer. —What news now

    With thy unhappy presence?

POGIO.

    O my lord, my Lord Vincentio is almost kill'd by my Lord

    Medice.

---

47. Honor] *Q corr.*; honour *Q*   58. Med'cines] *Q corr. (Medcines)*;
uncorr.   "*Medicines*" *Q uncorr.*

---

50. *late*] recent.
52. *fact*] deed.

STROZZA.

    See, doctor, see if my presage be true.   70
    And well I know, if he have hurt the prince,
    'Tis treacherously done, or with much help.

POGIO.

    Nay, sure he had no help but all the duke's guard; and
    they set upon him indeed, and after he had defended himself,
    d'ye see? he drew and, having as good as wounded the   75
    Lord Medice almost, he strake at him and miss'd him, d'ye
    mark?

STROZZA.

    What tale is here? Where is this mischief done?

POGIO.

    At Monk's-well, my lord; I'll guide you to him presently.

STROZZA.

    I doubt it not; fools are best guides to ill,   80
    And mischief's ready way lies open still.
    Lead, sir, I pray.   *Exeunt.*

[V.iii]   *Enter* Corteza *and* Margaret *above.*

CORTEZA.

    Quiet yourself niece; though your love be slain,
    You have another that's worth two of him.

MARGARET.

    It is not possible; it cannot be
    That heaven should suffer such impiety.

82. Lead . . . pray] *Q corr.*; *not in Q uncorr.*

---

    76. *strake*] struck.
    79. *Monk's-well*] a street in Cripplesgate, London, site of the Barber Surgeons' Hall, where dead bodies, especially those of executed criminals, were taken for dissection. Renaissance dramatists often allude to the hall as a grisly place (Sugden).
[V.iii]
    0.1. *above*] perhaps in one of two window stages which Smith says were located above the main-stage doors (p. 373), or perhaps merely in the gallery stage. Unconvincingly, Smith felt that, to "provide the necessary illusion of great height" for Margaret's proposed leap, a stage on still a higher level was "presumably used" (p. 414).

CORTEZA.
    'Tis true, I swear, niece.

MARGARET.   O most unjust truth!   5
    I'll cast myself down headlong from this tower
    And force an instant passage for my soul
    To seek the wand'ring spirit of my lord.

CORTEZA.
    Will you do so, niece? That I hope you will not.
    And yet there was a maid in St. Mark's Street   10
    For such a matter did so, and her clothes
    Flew up about her so as she had no harm;
    And, grace of God, your clothes may fly up too
    And save you harmless, for your cause and hers
    Are e'en as like as can be.

MARGARET.   I would not 'scape,   15
    And certainly I think the death is easy.

CORTEZA.
    O, 'tis the easiest death that ever was.
    Look, niece, it is so far hence to the ground
    You should be quite dead long before you felt it.
    Yet do not leap, niece.

MARGARET.   I will kill myself   20
    With running on some sword or drink strong poison;
    Which death is easiest I would fain endure.

CORTEZA.
    Sure, Cleopatra was of the same mind
    And did so; she was honor'd ever since.
    Yet do not you so, niece.   25

---

10. *St. Mark's Street*] There was in London a Mark Lane, sometimes called St. Mark's Lane, but Chapman probably had in mind the Piazza di San Marco in Venice (Sugden). Although his setting is unlocalized, it is in Italy, and the famous piazza was sometimes called St. Mark's Street in Renaissance dramas. (One scene of Marston's *Antonio's Revenge*, III.i, is set at "Saint Mark's Church.") The incident which Corteza describes is unknown but may have been narrated in some contemporary broadside or in an Italian novella; Sugden presumed that the maid had leaped from the Campanile of the church of San Marco.

23. *Cleopatra*] According to Plutarch's life of Mark Antony, Cleopatra tested poisons on condemned men to determine which would allow her the least painful suicide.

MARGARET.

    Wretch that I am, my heart is soft and faint

    And trembles at the very thought of death,

    Though thoughts tenfold more grievous do torment it.

    I'll feel death by degrees and first deform

    This my accursed face with ugly wounds,   30

    That was the first cause of my dear love's death.

CORTEZA.

    That were a cruel deed. Yet Adelasia,

    In Pettie's *Palace of Petite Pleasure*,

    For all the world with such a knife as this [*She produces a knife.*]

    Cut off her cheeks and nose and was commended   35

    More than all dames that kept their faces whole.

    O, do not cut it.   [Margaret *reaches for the knife.*]

MARGARET [*pulling back her hand*]. Fie on my faint heart;

    It will not give my hand the wished strength.

    Behold the just plague of a sensual life

    That, to preserve itself in reason's spite   40

    And shun death's horror, feels it ten times more.

    Unworthy women, why do men adore

    Our fading beauties when, their worthiest lives

    Being lost for us, we dare not die for them?

    Hence, hapless ornaments that adorn'd this head;   45

                             [*She disorders her hair.*]

    Disorder ever these enticing curls

    And leave my beauty like a wilderness

    That never man's eye more may dare t'invade.

---

46. enticing curls] *Shepherd*; entring
carles *Q* .

---

33. *Pettie's . . . Pleasure*] an English collection of Italianate novelle, *A Petite Palace of* [George] *Pettie his Pleasure* (1576). Corteza seems well read in such popular literature, but here either she or Chapman is confused. Although Pettie three times alludes to Adelasia, he does not tell her story, which involves a clandestine marriage aided by a gentlewoman attendant; Adelasia does not deform her face, and her story appears in an earlier collection of novelle, William Painter's *Palace of Pleasure* (1565–1566). Another tale told by Painter, that of Florinda, involves a mutilation only remotely similar to Margaret's. See Introduction, p. xvii.

    39. *sensual*] worldly, concerned with the senses.

    43. *fading*] transitory.

CORTEZA.

I'll tell you, niece—and yet I will not tell you
A thing that I desire to have you do, 50
But I will tell you only what you might do
'Cause I would pleasure you in all I could. [*She produces a jar.*]
I have an ointment here which we dames use
To take off hair when it does grow too low
Upon our foreheads, and that, for a need, 55
If you should rub it hard upon your face,
Would blister it and make it look most vilely.

MARGARET.

O give me that, aunt.

CORTEZA.

Give it you, virgin? That were well indeed;
Shall I be thought to tempt you to such matters? 60

MARGARET.

None, of my faith, shall know it. Gentle aunt,
Bestow it on me and I'll ever love you.

CORTEZA.

God's pity, but you shall not spoil your face.

MARGARET.

I will not, then, indeed.

CORTEZA.   Why then, niece, take it—
But you shall swear you will not.

MARGARET.   No, I swear. 65

[*She takes the ointment and smears her face.*]

CORTEZA.

What, do you force it from me? Gods my dear,
Will you misuse your face so? What, all over?
Nay, if you be so desp'rate, I'll be gone. *Exit.*

MARGARET.

Fade, hapless beauty, turn the ugliest face
That ever Ethiop or affrightful fiend 70
Show'd in th'amaz'd eye of prophan'd light.
See, precious love, if thou be yet in air

70. That] *Shepherd*; The *Q*.   72. yet] *Parrott*; it *Q*.

70. *affrightful*] terrifying.
72. *yet in air*] i.e., not yet arrived in heaven.

And canst break darkness and the strongest tow'rs
With thy dissolved intellectual pow'rs,
See a worse torment suffered for thy death   75
Than if it had extended his black force
In sevenfold horror to my hated life.
Smart, precious ointment, smart, and to my brain
Sweat thy envenom'd fury; make my eyes
Burn with thy sulphur like the lakes of hell,   80
That fear of me may shiver him to dust
That eat his own child with the jaws of lust.   [*Exit.*]

[V.iv]   *Enter* Alphonso, Lasso, *and others.*

ALPHONSO.
I wonder how far they pursu'd my son,
That no return of him or them appears.
I fear some hapless accident is chanc'd
That makes the news so loath to pierce mine ears.

LASSO.
High heaven vouchsafe no such effect succeed   5
Those wretched causes that from my house flow,
But that in harmless love all acts may end.

Enter Corteza.

CORTEZA.
What shall I do? Alas, I cannot rule
My desperate niece. All her sweet face is spoil'd,
And I dare keep her prisoner no more.   10
See, see, she comes frantic and all undress'd.

Enter Margaret.

82. S.D. *Exit*] *Parrott*; *Exeunt Q* .

73–75.] i.e., if his disembodied mind (soul) can penetrate the darkness
of death and the walls of her tower.
76. *it*] death.
79. *Sweat*] cause to penetrate.
82. *eat*] ate. The allusion is presumably to Saturn (in Greek, Cronos),
but the indirect allusion to Alphonso is more important.

MARGARET.

    Tyrant! Behold how thou hast us'd thy love.
    See, thief to Nature, thou hast kill'd and robb'd,
    Kill'd what myself kill'd, robb'd what makes thee poor.
    Beauty, a lover's treasure, thou hast lost   15
    Where none can find it; all a poor maid's dow'r
    Thou hast forc'd from me, all my joy and hope:
    No man will love me more; all dames excel me.
    This ugly thing is now no more a face,
    Nor any vile form in all earth resembled   20
    But thy foul tyranny, for which all the pains
    Two faithful lovers feel that thus are parted,
    All joys they might have felt turn all to pains,
    All a young virgin thinks she does endure
    To lose her love and beauty, on thy heart   25
    Be heap'd and press'd down till thy soul depart.

Enter Julio.

JULIO.

    Haste, liege, your son is dangerously hurt.
    Lord Medice, contemning your command,
    By me delivered as your highness will'd,
    Set on him with your guard, who struck him down;   30
    And then the coward lord with mortal wounds
    And slavish insolency plow'd up his soft breast,
    Which barbarous fact in part is laid on you
    For first enjoining it, and foul exclaims
    In pity of your son your subjects breathe   35

12. Tyrant!] *Q corr.*; Tyrant, *Q uncorr.*
14. poor.] *Q corr.* (poore); poore, *Q uncorr.*
15. lost] *Q corr.*; lost, *Q uncorr.*
16. maid's] *Q corr.* (Maides); Maide *Q uncorr.*
16. dow'r] *Q uncorr.* (dowre); dowre: *Q corr.*
17. me,] *Parrott 1*; me: *Q corr.*; me; *Q uncorr., Parrott.*
17. hope:] *this edn.*; hope. *Q corr.*; hope, *Q uncorr.*

---

26. *Be . . . down*] She wants his heart to be burdened with (1) the *pains* of the separated lovers, (2) the sense of loss in that anticipated *joys* have become pains, and (3) the special sense of loss that a young girl feels at the loss of *her love and beauty*.
    33. *fact*] deed.
    34. *exclaims*] exclamations.

'Gainst your unnatural fury; amongst whom
The good Lord Strozza desp'rately raves,
And vengeance for his friend's injustice craves.
See where he comes, burning in zeal of friendship.

Enter Strozza, Vincentio *brought in a chair*, Benevenius, Pogio,
Cynanche, *with a* Guard, Strozza *before, and* Medice.

STROZZA.
    Where is the tyrant? Let me strike his eyes   40
    Into his brain with horror of an object.—
    See, pagan Nero, see how thou hast ripp'd
    Thy better bosom, rooted up that flow'r
    From whence thy now spent life should spring anew,
    And in him kill'd, that would have bred thee fresh,   45
    Thy mother and thy father.
VINCENTIO.   Good friend, cease.
STROZZA.
    What hag with child of monster would have nurs'd
    Such a prodigious longing? But a father
    Would rather eat the brawn out of his arms
    Than glut the mad worm of his wild desires   50
    With his dear issue's entrails.
VINCENTIO.   Honor'd friend,
    He is my father and he is my prince,
    In both whose rights he may command my life.
STROZZA.
    What is a father? Turn his entrails gulfs
    To swallow children when they have begot them?   55
    And what's a prince? Had all been virtuous men,
    There never had been prince upon the earth

37. desp'rately] *Q corr.*; desparately   *meant for* desparate, *l. 9, on the same*
Q uncorr. (*but perhaps the correction was*   *page in Q*).

42. *Nero*] Nero murdered his mother, as Alphonso, by killing his son,
has in effect killed his mother and father (ll. 43–46). "The point of the
conceit lies in the Elizabethan commonplace that a man lived again in his
children and descendants" (Parrott).

47. *of*] by a.

54. *Turn . . . gulfs*] do his internal parts turn into chasms. Strozza
alludes to Saturn, who swallowed his children (Parrott). Cf. V.iii.82.

56. *virtuous*] strong. The idea expressed here is characteristic of Chapman's
plays.

And so no subject: all men had been princes.
A virtuous man is subject to no prince
But to his soul and honor, which are laws   60
That carry fire and sword within themselves,
Never corrupted, never out of rule.
What is there in a prince that his least lusts
Are valued at the lives of other men,
When common faults in him should prodigies be   65
And his gross dotage rather loath'd than sooth'd?

ALPHONSO.

How thick and heavily my plagues descend,
Not giving my 'maz'd pow'rs a time to speak!
Pour more rebuke upon me, worthy lord,
For I have guilt and patience for them all.—   70
Yet know, dear son, I did forbid thy harm;
This gentleman can witness, whom I sent
With all command of haste to interdict
This forward man in mischief not to touch thee.—
Did I not, Julio? Utter nought but truth.   75

JULIO.

All your guard heard, my lord, I gave your charge
With loud and violent iterations,
After all which Lord Medice cowardly hurt him.

THE GUARD.

He did, my princely lord.

ALPHONSO.   Believe then, son,
And know me pierc'd as deeply with thy wounds.— 80
And pardon, virtuous lady, that have lost
The dearest treasure proper to your sex,
Ay me, it seems by my unhappy means!
O would to God I could, with present cure
Of these unnatural wounds and moaning right   85

---

63. least] *Q corr.*; lest *Q uncorr.* *Parrott 1 reports suggested emendations*
85. moaning right] *Q* (moning); *to* moving (*cf. II.i.194*) *and to* sight.

---

65. *common . . . be*] Faults which are common to all are magnified into prodigies in a prince.

74. *forward . . . mischief*] man eager to do mischief.

85. *unnatural . . . right*] Vincentio's wounds, unnatural because inflicted by a father; Margaret's justified lamentation (Parrott) or her just cause which is *moaning* because of my interference.

Of this abused beauty, join you both,
As last I left you, in eternal nuptials.

VINCENTIO.

My lord, I know the malice of this man,
Not your unkind consent, hath us'd us thus.
And since I make no doubt I shall survive   90
These fatal dangers, and your grace is pleas'd
To give free course to my unwounded love,
'Tis not this outward beauty's ruthful loss
Can any thought discourage my desires.—
And therefore, dear life, do not wrong me so   95
To think my love the shadow of your beauty.
I woo your virtues, which as I am sure
No accident can alter or impair,
So be you certain nought can change my love.

MARGARET.

I know your honorable mind, my lord,   100
And will not do it that unworthy wrong
To let it spend her forces in contending,
Spite of your sense, to love me thus deformed:
Love must have outward objects to delight him,
Else his content will be too grave and sour.   105
It is enough for me, my lord, you love,
And that my beauty's sacrifice redeem'd
My sad fear of your slaughter. You first lov'd me
Closely for beauty, which being wither'd thus,
Your love must fade. When the most needful rights   110
Of Fate and Nature have dissolv'd your life
And that your love must needs be all in soul,
Then will we meet again; and then, dear love,
Love me again, for then will beauty be
Of no respect with love's eternity.   115

107. beauty's] *Shepherd*; beauties *Q*.

89. *unkind*] unnatural.
96. *shadow*] image; i.e., his love does not suffer defacement as her beauty
has.
102. *contending*] striving, trying hard.
103. *Spite . . . sense*] despite your sense (of sight).
105. *content*] satisfaction, happiness.
109. *Closely*] secretly.
115. *respect*] consideration.

VINCENTIO.

    Nor is it now: I wooed your beauty first
    But as a lover; now as a dear husband
    That title and your virtues bind me ever.

MARGARET.

    Alas, that title is of little force
    To stir up men's affections; when wives want   120
    Outward excitements, husbands' loves grow scant.

BENEVENIUS.

    Assist me, heaven; and art, give me your mask;

                [*He opens his casket and removes a mask and medicines.*]

    Open, thou little storehouse of great Nature;
    Use an elixir drawn through seven years' fire
    That, like Medea's cauldron, can repair   125
    The ugliest loss of living temp'rature,
    And for this princely pair of virtuous turtles
    Be lavish of thy precious influence.—
    Lady, t'attone your honorable strife
    And take all let from your love's tender eyes,   130
    Let me forever hide this stain of beauty
    With this recureful mask.

        [*He applies the mask to* Margaret'*s face.*]

              Here be it fix'd
    With painless operation; of itself,
    Your beauty having brook'd three days' eclipse,
    Like a dissolved cloud it shall fall off,   135
    And your fair looks regain their freshest rays.

---

120. affections] *Shepherd*; affectious
Q .
122. heaven; . . . art,] *Shepherd*;
Heauen, . . . Art, *Q* ; Heaven
. . . Art! *Parrott*.

128–130. influence. . . . eyes,]
Shepherd; influence . . . eyes. *Q* .

---

    118. *title*] i.e., *husband*.

    122. *art*] human knowledge (of medicine). Parrott, however, thought that heaven and art were to assist Benevenius, and one of the ladies present was to give him her mask.

    125. *Medea's cauldron*] "Medea by means of her magic cauldron restored youth to the aged father of Jason" (Parrott).

    126.] "The most serious damage to a living being's constitution" (Parrott).

    127. *turtles*] turtle-doves, emblematic of true and constant love.

So shall your princely friend, if heaven consent,
In twice your suffer'd date renew recure.
Let me then have the honor to conjoin
Your hands, conformed to your constant hearts.   140

ALPHONSO.

Grave Benevenius, honorable doctor,
On whose most sovereign Aesculapian hand
Fame with her richest miracles attends,
Be fortunate, as ever heretofore,
That we may 'quite thee, both with gold and honor,   145
And by thy happy means have pow'r to make
My son and his much-injur'd love amends,
Whose well-proportion'd choice we now applaud
And bless all those that ever further'd it.—
[*To* Lasso.]   Where is your discreet usher, my good lord,   150
The special furtherer of this equal match?

JULIO.

Brought after by a couple of your guard.

ALPHONSO.

Let him be fetch'd that we may do him grace.

POGIO.

I'll fetch him, my lord; away you must not go. O, here he
comes.—   155

[*Enter* Bassiolo *guarded.*]

O master usher, I am sorry for you; you must presently be
chopp'd in pieces.

BASSIOLO.

Woe to that wicked prince that e'er I saw him.

POGIO.

Come, come, I gull you, master usher. You are like to be the
duke's minion, man. D'ye think I would have been seen in   160
your company and you had been out of favor? —Here's
my friend master usher, my lord.

155.1. *Enter* Bassiolo *guarded*] *Parrott*;
not in Q .

138.] be cured again in six days.
140. *conformed to*] put into the same form as (i.e., joined together).
142. *Aesculapian*] like Aesculapius, Greek god of medicine.

ALPHONSO.

> Give me your hand, friend. Pardon us, I pray;
> We much have wrong'd your worth as one that knew
> The fitness of this match above ourselves. 165

BASSIOLO.

> Sir, I did all things for the best, I swear,
> And you must think I would not have been gull'd.
> I know what's fit, sir, as I hope you know now.—
> Sweet Vince, how far'st thou? Be of honor'd cheer.

LASSO.

> Vince does he call him? —O fool, dost thou call 170
> The prince Vince like his equal?

BASSIOLO.   O my lord, alas,

> You know not what has pass'd 'twixt us two.—
> [*Embracing* Vincentio.]   Here in thy bosom I will lie, sweet
>   Vince,
> And die if thou die, I protest by heaven.

LASSO.

> I know not what this means.

ALPHONSO.   Nor I, my lord, 175

> But sure he saw the fitness of the match
> With freer and more noble eyes than we.

POGIO.

> Why, I saw that as well as he, my lord; I knew 'twas a
> foolish match betwixt you two. —Did not you think so,
> my Lord Vincentio? —Lord uncle, did not I say at first 180
> of the duke, "Will his antiquity never leave his iniquity?"

STROZZA.

> Go to, too much of this. But ask this lord
> If he did like it.

POGIO.   Who, my Lord Medice?

STROZZA.

> Lord Stinkard, man, his name is. Ask him, "Lord Stinkard,
> did you like the match?" Say. 185

POGIO.

> My lord Stinkard, did you like the match betwixt the duke
> and my lady Margaret?

184. Stinkard, man] *Shepherd*;
"*Stinkard Man*" Q .

MEDICE [*drawing his sword*].

    Presumptuous sycophant, I will have thy life.

ALPHONSO.

    Unworthy lord, put up. Thirst'st thou more blood?

    Thy life is fitt'st to be call'd in question   190

    For thy most murd'rous cowardice on my son.

    Thy forwardness to every cruelty

    Calls thy pretended noblesse in suspect.

STROZZA.

    Noblesse, my lord? Set by your princely favor

    That gave the luster to his painted state,   195

    Who ever view'd him but with deep contempt,

    As reading vileness in his very looks?

    And if he prove not son of some base drudge

    Trimm'd up by Fortune, being dispos'd to jest

    And dally with your state, then that good angel   200

    That by divine relation spake in me,

    Foretelling these foul dangers to your son,

    And without notice brought this reverend man

    To rescue him from death now fails my tongue,

    And I'll confess I do him open wrong.   205

MEDICE.

    And so thou dost, and I return all note

    Of infamy or baseness on thy throat.

    Damn me, my lord, if I be not a lord.

STROZZA.

    My liege, with all desert even now you said

    His life was duly forfeit for the death   210

    Which in these barbarous wounds he sought your son.

    Vouchsafe me then his life in my friend's right,

    For many ways, I know, he merits death,

    Which, if you grant, will instantly appear,

    And that I feel with some rare miracle.   215

ALPHONSO.

    His life is thine, Lord Strozza; give him death.

---

193. *in suspect*] into suspicion.
194. *Set by*] except for.
199. *Trimm'd*] dressed.
211. *sought*] sought for.
214. *Which*] refers to the *many ways* in which he merits death.

MEDICE.

    What, my lord!

    Will your grace cast away an innocent life?

STROZZA.

    Villain, thou liest; thou guilty art of death

    A hundred ways, which now I'll execute.   220

                                       [He draws his sword.]

MEDICE [*to* Alphonso].

    Recall your word, my lord.

ALPHONSO.   Not for the world.

STROZZA.

    O my dear liege, but that my spirit prophetic

    Hath inward feeling of such sins in him

    As ask the forfeit of his life and soul,

    I would before I took his life give leave   225

    To his confession and his penitence:

    O, he would tell you most notorious wonders

    Of his most impious state. But life and soul

    Must suffer for it in him, and my hand

    Forbidden is from heaven to let him live   230

    Till by confession he may have forgiveness.—

    Die, therefore, monster.

VINCENTIO.

    O, be not so uncharitable, sweet friend.

    Let him confess his sins and ask heaven pardon.

STROZZA.

    He must not, princely friend; it is heaven's justice   235

    To plague his life and soul, and here's heaven's justice.

                                   [Threatening Medice.]

MEDICE [*to* Lasso].

    O save my life, my lord.

LASSO.   Hold, good Lord Strozza;

    Let him confess the sins that heaven hath told you

    And ask forgiveness.

MEDICE [*to* Strozza].   Let me, good my lord,

    And I'll confess what you accuse me of,   240

    Wonders indeed and full of damn'd deserts.

230–231. *live . . . forgiveness*] i.e., live long enough to confess and be forgiven.

STROZZA.

    I know it, and I must not let thee live
    To ask forgiveness.

ALPHONSO.   But you shall, my lord,
    Or I will take his life out of your hand.

STROZZA.

    A little then I am content, my liege.—   245
    Is thy name Medice?

MEDICE.   No, my noble lord;
    My true name is Mendice.

STROZZA.   Mendice! See,
    At first a mighty scandal done to honor.—
    Of what country art thou?

MEDICE.   Of no country I,
    But born upon the seas, my mother passing   250
    'Twixt Zant and Venice.

STROZZA.

    Where wert thou christen'd?

MEDICE.   I was never christen'd,
    But, being brought up with beggars, call'd Mendice.

ALPHONSO.

    Strange and unspeakable.

STROZZA.   How cam'st thou then
    To bear that port thou didst, ent'ring this court?   255

MEDICE.

    My lord, when I was young, being able limb'd,
    A captain of the gypsies entertain'd me,
    And many years I liv'd a loose life with them.
    At last I was so favor'd that they made me
    The king of gypsies; and, being told my fortune   260
    By an old sorceress, that I should be great

254. Strange] *Q uncorr.*; Strange,
Q corr.

---

248. *At first*] from the first. The scandal is the usurping of a noble name,
that of the Medicis.

251. *Zant*] an island in the Ionian sea, famous for its wooded fertility
and its pitch-wells.

257. *gypsies*] There was official concern about gypsies; in 1601, two
women were convicted of associating with gypsies, and one of them was
hanged (G. B. Harrison, *The Elizabethan Journals* [London, 1938], III, 155).

In some great prince's love, I took the treasure
Which all our company of gypsies had
In many years, by several stealths, collected,
And, leaving them in wars, I liv'd abroad   265
With no less show than now. And my last wrong
I did to noblesse was in this high court.

ALPHONSO.

Never was heard so strange a counterfeit.

STROZZA.

Didst thou not cause me to be shot in hunting?

MEDICE.

I did, my lord, for which, for heaven's love, pardon.   270

STROZZA.

Now let him live, my lord: his blood's least drop
Would stain your court more than the sea could cleanse;
His soul's too foul to expiate with death.

ALPHONSO.

Hence, then, be ever banish'd from my rule,
And live a monster, loath'd of all the world.   275

POGIO.

I'll get boys and bait him out o'th' court, my lord.

ALPHONSO.

Do so, I pray thee; rid me of his sight.

POGIO.

Come on, my lord Stinkard; I'll play fox, fox, come out of
thy hole with you, i'faith.

MEDICE.

I'll run and hide me from the sight of heaven.   280

POGIO.

Fox, fox, go out of thy hole; a two-legg'd fox,
A two-legg'd fox.   *Exit with pages beating* Medice.

BENEVENIUS.

Never was such an accident disclos'd.

ALPHONSO.

Let us forget it, honorable friends,
And satisfy all wrongs with my son's right   285
In solemn marriage of his love and him.

278–279. *fox . . . hole*] a Christmas game "in which boys beat each other
with gloves or bits of leather tied to strings" (Parrott).

VINCENTIO.

    I humbly thank your highness. —Honor'd doctor,
    The balsam you infus'd into my wounds
    Hath eas'd me much and given me sudden strength
    Enough t'assure all danger is exempt   290
    That any way may let the general joy
    My princely father speaks of in our nuptials.

ALPHONSO.

    Which, my dear son, shall with thy full recure
    Be celebrate in greater majesty
    Than ever grac'd our greatest ancestry.   295
    Then take thy love, which heaven with all joys bless
    And make ye both mirrors of happiness.

FINIS

---

   290. *exempt*] removed.
   294.] See Introduction, p. xxxii, and cf. the significant pun (*right–rite*)
in l. 285.

Appendix A

The Source of the Strozza Plot

In the Introduction, I have analyzed Chapman's use of Chapter X of Antonio Benivieni's *De Abditis Nonnullis ac Mirandis Morborum & Sanationum Causis Liber*. The work was published posthumously at Florence in 1507, edited by the author's brother Girolamo; it was reprinted (in volumes containing other medical works) at Venice in 1516, at Harderwijk in 1521, at Basel in 1528 and 1529, and at Cologne in 1581.[1] I have examined the British Museum copies of all these editions and have found no substantial variants among them. I present below the text of Chapter X from the 1581 edition, which was appended to *Medicinalivm Obseruationum Exempla Rara, Recognita & Aucta* (pp. 152–154), a similar work by the famous Dutch physician and botanist, Rembert Dodoens. Following the text I present my own English translation.[2]

Miraculo liberatus

Ivvenis quidam Florentinus nomine Gaspar, dum circa praecordia sagitta vulneratus spiculum educere nititur, relicto mucrone arundinem tantum euellit. Quem cum chirurgici, omni licet ingenio, omnique praesidio nixi, auellere minime potuerint (in intima enim costa adeo insedarat, vt reuelli nullo auxilio posset, nisi costa ipsa perfracta, & vulnere ampliore facto) mortem potius quamlibet miserabilem, quam tale genus curationis subire malebat. Quare

---

[1] The 1507 edition is available in facsimile, with a slightly inaccurate translation by Charles Singer (Springfield, Ill., 1954); Esmond R. Long's preface on "Antonio Benivieni and His Contribution to Pathological Anatomy" (pp. xviii–xlvi) is useful. Benivieni's work had previously been translated into Italian by Carlo Burci in 1843.

[2] The text and (in substantially identical form) the translation appeared in my article "The Genesis of the Strozza Subplot in George Chapman's *The Gentleman Usher*," *Publications of the Modern Language Association*, LXXXIII (1968), 1449–1450.

tandem in desperationem versus, laqueo suspendere se, aut profluenti Arno, vel alto puteo praecipitem dare cogitabat: quod & fecisset, nisi assistentes amici illum diligentissime custodissent. Inter quos erat vir quidam Marioctus nomine, fide & probitate pollens: hic hominem iugiter deprecabatur, vt desperatione reiecta, in manus potius Dei, a quo est omnis salus, tam grande malum tradere conaretur. Huius tandem precibus flexus Gaspar totus ad Deum conuertitur, non die, non nocte ab oratione cessans: donec in vaticinium prorumpens, nonnullos interim, qui ad eum visendi gratia accederent, dum adhuc procul essent, paulo post adfuturos praediceret. Quinetiam & ignotum quemlibet proprio quoque nomine citans, admonebat astantes omnes vti Deum timerent, & de salute sua confiderent. Se enim non modo de ea, deque die & hora qua illam consequi deberet, certiorem factum esse, sed multa praeter ea eodem lumine praeuidisse aiebat: vt profectionem suam Romam & mortem, exilium Petri Medicis & fugam, ciuitatis nostrae Florentinae angustias & calamitates, Italiae subuersionem & alia quamplurima, quae breuitatis causa silentio praeterimus: quaeque fere omnia magna ex parte impleta iam videmus. Nam,& qua praedixerat die atque hora mucro ipso ex vulnere sponte sua prosilijt: quo eiecto etiam vaticinari destitit, & Roman tandem peregre proficiscens mortuus est.

Cured by a Miracle

A certain Florentine youth named Gaspar was wounded around the midriff with an arrow; when he tried to remove it, the shaft came out, leaving the arrowhead behind. Physicians who tried could not extract it despite their every talent and their every effort: it had imbedded itself so firmly in his deepest rib that it could not be removed by any method unless the rib itself were broken and the wound made larger. Gaspar preferred death, however miserable, over submitting to that kind of cure. Becoming desperate at last, he considered hanging himself, or throwing himself into the River Arno, or casting himself headlong into a deep well; he would have killed himself if the friends around him had not watched him very carefully. Among these friends was a certain man named Marioctus, outstanding in faith and probity; he continually begged Gaspar to stop being desperate and to try submitting his great illness into the hands of God, from whom all health derives. Gaspar was finally won over by his entreaties and turned himself wholly to God. Day and night he prayed without ceasing. At length he broke into prophecies: he predicted, while they were still far away, that some people would be arriving soon who were already on their way to visit him. He called even strangers by their proper names. He warned all those around him to fear God and to have faith in his recovery; he said he had been assured of that, and of the day and hour on which he would recover. He said, moreover, that he had foreseen many things according to the same light: his own trip to Rome and his death, the exile and flight of Piero de' Medici, the straits and calamities of our Florentine city, the ruin of Italy, and many other things which for the sake of brevity I pass over in silence.[3] Almost all these things were for the most part fulfilled. For even on the day and the hour which he predicted, the arrowhead sprang forth of its own accord. As soon as it was out, he stopped prophesying. In the end, going abroad to Rome, he died.

[3] Piero de' Medici ruled Florence from 1492 until forced to flee by citizens enraged over his acceptance of humiliating peace terms from the French king Charles VIII in 1494. Thereafter Florence suffered from a chaotic vacuum of leadership only partially filled by Savonarola's republican reforms. All Italy was rent from within during this period by factionalism and corruption of church and state, and French invasions brought repeated disasters for nearly twenty years.

Appendix B

Pogio's Dreams

In the first scene of *The Gentleman Usher*, Pogio recounts two dreams the substance and the narration of which mark him as a dolt. The narratives are in fact *facetiae*, droll stories of a type very popular for centuries. Although many important writers are known at least in part for their *facetiae*, including Rabelais, Castiglione, and Henri Estienne, one of the most popular was a Florentine classical scholar and lay official of the church, Poggio Bracciolini. His *Facetiae* were often reprinted, and, though I have found none which could have supplied Chapman with the materials of Pogio's dreams, the Italian author could conceivably have suggested to Chapman the name of his character.

The source of Pogio's second dream, in which he spent the night tying Margaret's shoestrings, has not been found, but F. L. Schoell identified the source of his dream about the curtal horse in a work which also supplied material for *Sir Giles Goosecap* (Parrott, *The Comedies*, p. 894 n.). The *facetia* is in Estienne Tabourot's *Apophtegmes dv S. Gavlard Gentil-homme de la Franche-Comté Bourguignotte*, which is appended to some editions of Tabourot's *Les Bigarrvres dv Seignevr des Accords*, a miscellaneous collection of essays on various subjects. Sieur Gaulard was a fictitious dolt, and Seigneur des Accords was a pseudonym for Tabourot, a popular poet and wit born in Dijon in 1549 and said to have written the *Apophtegmes* to satirize the inhabitants of Franche-Comté. I quote the tale from the edition at Lyons, 1599, f. 106:

> Il [Sieur Gaulard] fit bretauder l'vn de ses cheuaux, puis ayant ouy dire que le sieur d'Engouleuent se plaignoit d'vn courtant bretaudé, qu'on luy auoit desrobbé n'agueres, & qu'il menaçoit de rompre bras & iambes au larron: Hé! mon amy, dit-il au mareschal, qu'il manda expressément, sçauez vous qu'il y a, remettez vn peu la queuë & les aureilles à mon cheual, afin que monsieur d'Engouleuent ne pense pas que ce soit le sien.

APPENDIX B

One J. B. of Charterhouse translated some of Tabourot's tales about the time of the Restoration, and his manuscript was finally printed more than two centuries later: *Bigarrures or The Pleasant and Witlesse and Simple Speeches of the Lord Gaulard of Burgundy from a Manuscript circa 1660* (Glasgow, 1884). I quote J. B.'s English version of Tabourot's tale from that edition, p. 16:

> He made one of his Horses to be Curtaild and his eares cut, and heareing that Monsieur d'Engouleuent had a Curtald horse stolen from him not long agoe and threatned to breake the Armes and Leggs of [him] that stole him. He sent for his ffarrier and commanded him expresly to put on againe the taile and the eares of his horse, least Monsieur d'Engouleuent should thinke that it was his horse.

Appendix C

The Gentleman Usher

Although Bassiolo is, from beginning to end, a dupe with an "overweening thought of his own worth," and, occasional expressions of pity notwithstanding, an object of derision, we should understand that his office was by no means insignificant. The office of gentleman usher in a Renaissance household was an ancient and important one, second only to that of the steward (in noble households) or chamberlain (in the royal household). Servants in these top ranks were not menials and traditionally did not come from the commonalty: Renaissance noblemen were accustomed to being served by the sons and daughters of gentlemen or other noblemen. I. M., the unknown author of *A Health to the Gentlemanly Profession of Serving-Men*, described the ideal:

> Amongst what sort of people should then this Seruing-man be sought for: Euen the Dukes sonne preferred Page to the Prince, the Earles seconde sonne attendant vpon the Duke, the Knights seconde sonne the Earles Seruant, the Esquires sonne to weare the Knightes lyuerie, and the Gentlemans sonne the Esquiers Seruingmen.[1]

Often, in fact, servants were of the same social rank as their masters. Ideally, the servant was expected to have courtly qualifications as well as social rank: I. M. listed courage, wit, discretion, self-control, and excellence in sports, shooting, dancing, and the like. The identities of specific servants in Renaissance households, even in the royal household, are only occasionally preserved, but some of the known names indicate that at court the ideal was often met at least as to social rank: in 1526 two gentlemen ushers to Henry VIII were the

[1] (London, 1598), sigs. B2v–B3. The work has been reprinted, with an Introduction by A. V. Judges, in the Shakespeare Association Facsimiles, No. 3 (Oxford, 1931).

diplomat Sir Philip Hobby and another knight, Sir Morris Barkley;[2] and when James I made provision in 1610 for the establishment of a household for the young prince Henry, he named as gentlemen ushers two knights, Sir Robert Darcy and Sir William Erwine.[3] Probably some of these royal appointments were merely sinecures, like that which John Gay declined in 1727 when George II offered to make him gentleman usher to the young princess Louisa.[4] Jonathan Swift mockingly described what Gay's duties would have been:

> Say, had the Court no better place to chuse
> For thee, than make a dry Nurse of thy Muse?
> How cheaply had thy Liberty been sold,
> To squire a Royal Girl of two Years old!
> In Leading strings her Infant-steps to guide;
> Or, with her Go-Cart amble Side by Side.[5]

But at least some of the gentlemen ushers were working servants, and they were important figures in the functioning of the household:

[2] *A Collection of Ordinances and Regulations for the Government of the Royal Household, Made in Divers Reigns. From King Edward III. to King William and Queen Mary* (London, 1790), p. 165. The full title of the office is Gentleman Usher of the Privy Chamber (to be distinguished from the rather more personal office of Gentleman of the Privy Chamber); there were other gentlemen ushers of the outer chambers, as well as several ushers of yeoman rank. The number of gentlemen ushers of the privy chamber varied from household to household and even from time to time: Elizabeth had five in about 1578 (ibid., p. 250) and eighteen in 1593 (B. M. Harl. MS. 1848, f. 25); James I had four, apparently the most common number for monarchs, in at least one list (B. M. Harl. MS. 6381, f. 16ᵛ); Catherine Bertie, Baroness Willoughby and Duchess Dowager of Suffolk, had three in 1560–1562 (M. St. Clare Byrne, "The Social Background," in *A Companion to Shakespeare Studies*, ed. Harley Granville-Barker and G. B. Harrison [Cambridge, 1934], p. 210); Anthony Browne, Viscount Montague, in 1595 seems customarily to have had one but made provision for an occasional second "for increase of state," i.e., for show ("A Booke of Orders and Rules," ed. S. D. Scott, *Sussex Archaeological Collections*, VII [1854], 195).

[3] *A Collection of Ordinances*, p. 323. For other gentlemen ushers identified by name at various dates see pp. 154, 167, and 250.

[4] *The Works of Alexander Pope*, ed. Whitwell Elwin and W. J. Courthope, Vol. VII: *The Correspondence*, II (London, 1871), 103. Similarly, Chapman's own appointment (*c.* 1604) as sewer in ordinary to Prince Henry seems to have been a form of literary patronage, to support Chapman's translation of Homer.

[5] "To Mr. Gay," *The Poems of Jonathan Swift*, ed. Harold Williams, II (Oxford, 1937), 531. In "A Libel on D— D—" Swift wrote about one who "Rejects a servile *Usher*'s Place,/ And leaves *St. James*'s in disgrace."

although the rank of one "Clarke, the gentleman usher" of Queen Elizabeth is not known, his death in 1602 was thought worthy of record by the gossip John Chamberlain in a letter to Dudley Carleton, Secretary to the Ambassador in France.[6]

The ideal of rank was probably less commonly upheld in non-royal households, even though "the king's house . . . is the requisite to be the mirrour of others."[7] The main thrust of I. M.'s work, previously quoted, is that "the death and decay of Liberalitie or Reward for well doing" and the "compounding of this pure and refined mettall (whereof Seruingmen were first formed) with untryed dregges and drosse of lesse esteeme" had debased the quality of service so much that even farmers' sons were usurping the best positions.[8] As early as 1552, Catherine Baroness Willoughby, Duchess Dowager of Suffolk, had as a gentleman usher Richard Bertie, the "meanly born" son of a stonemason, "in the lowest rank of the social scale."[9] But the circumstances were somewhat unusual: through important connections and through his wit Bertie had received an Oxford education; perhaps through the influence of the duchess, his father had been preferred to the captaincy of Hurst Castle with a coat-or-arms; and Catherine then married her gentleman usher.

In fact, the office of gentleman usher conveyed gentle status upon its incumbent even if he did not have that status by birth. The situation as described somewhat later by William Bird was just as much present in the early 1600's:

> . . . in these dayes he is a Gentleman, who is so commonly taken, and reputed . . . whosoever studieth in the Vniversities, who professeth the liberall sciences, and to be short, who can live idly, and without manuall labour, and will bear the Port,

[6] *Calendar of State Papers (Domestic) . . . 1601–1603* (London, 1870), p. 269. This Clarke could be the same one who carried a letter between the same correspondents in 1598 (*Calendar of State Papers [Domestic] . . . 1598–1601* [London, 1869], p. 51). Could he also be the Thomas Clarke who was a Messenger of the Privy Council in 1601? (See *Acts of the Privy Council of England*, n.s. XXX [London, 1905], 308, 416, 436; XXXII [London, 1907], 19, 281.)

[7] Paul V. B. Jones, *The Household of a Tudor Nobleman*, University of Illinois Studies in the Social Sciences, VI (Urbana, 1917), 22, quoting an order by Henry VIII; see also Byrne, p. 203.

[8] I. M., sig. C3 *et passim*.

[9] Cecilie Goff, *A Woman of the Tudor Age* (London, 1930), pp. 212–214.

charge, and countenance of a Gentleman, he shall bee called Master.[10]

Bassiolo is called master, but his rank by birth is not clearly indicated. Margaret calls him squire (III.ii.380, IV.v.39), the rank just below knighthood, but she is using the title condescendingly and perhaps not literally. Bassiolo's audacity in calling Vincentio Vince astounds both Margaret and Lasso, but even a nobleman would have been considered audacious in being so familiar with the prince. Bassiolo does not seem socially distinguished, and he clearly wants such qualifications as I. M. demanded in a serving-man. But he is a man of means: from his salary as gentleman usher,[11] he has invested in (or perhaps he receives as perquisites the income from) lands worth some £375 (III.ii.42).

Whatever his rank, a gentleman usher was expected to be well versed in social proprieties. He was "probably the most active man in the entire household personnel,"[12] and surviving household statutes make clear that he was a very busy man indeed. Subordinate to the steward or chamberlain, he supervised every detail of the preparation and serving of meals, from the washing of the waiters' hands to the delicate task of arranging the seating; often assisted in the dressing of his master; was responsible for the performance of all the household servants and often for hiring and firing them; oversaw the cleaning and furnishing of rooms; assigned lodgings to guests; announced callers; led the way when his master proceeded through the country or the city; and in general stood ready to fulfill any command at home or abroad. Typically, Viscount Montague gave his gentleman usher summary authority, "in cyvill and kynde manner to comaunde any gentleman or yeoman to doe any service that shalbe for myne honor, and [anyone] who shall in such case disobeye him shall

[10] *The Magazine of Honour* (London, 1642), sig. N6. Bird also enjoined, "If one be a Gentleman by office, and looseth his office, then he doth also lose his gentility" (sig. N7v).

[11] At court his salary would have been £30 annually plus perquisites amounting to full subsistence, not to mention tips (E. K. Chambers, *The Elizabethan Stage* [Oxford, 1923], I, 50; *A Collection of Ordinances*, pp. 169, 250, 321). In non-royal households it would presumably have been lower: A. V. Judges speaks of the "customary 13s. 4d. a quarter [£2 13s. 4d. annually] with livery earned by gentlemen ushers and waiters" (Shakespeare Association Facsimile, No. 3, p. x), but he may have been speaking of the gentlemen ushers of the outer chamber.

[12] Jones, p. 155.

nott serve me butt uppon his especiall suyte made unto me in his behalfe."[13] At court, when an entertainment was scheduled, it was the monarch's gentleman usher, under the chamberlain, who supervised the "'apparelling' of the room" and who "seated the audience, kept the doors against the turbulent crowds knocking for admission, cleared the dancing-place when the King was seated, and supplied the principal guests with programmes or abstracts of the device prepared by the poet."[14] The procedure would presumably have been very similar for entertainments in a nobleman's household. Bassiolo is as important in Earl Lasso's household as any gentleman usher governed by the statutes summarized above. During the first three acts of *The Gentleman Usher*, he is seen performing many of the tasks listed there: ordering servants about, apparelling the room and directing the players for an entertainment, leading a procession, having the power to discharge Fungus, and so on. In two places he is called "Superintendent" in the uncorrected readings of the quarto, and Lasso expressly states his importance: "you on whom relies/ The general disposition of my house/ In this our preparation for the duke" (I.ii.2–4). He does it all with too much officiousness and self-importance: "His place is great, for he's not only/ My father's [Lasso's] usher, but the world's beside" (IV.ii.117–118). Because of his vanity, Vincentio's purposeful flattery of him as "the festival robe/ That made [Lord Lasso] show so glorious and divine" (III.ii. 31–32) falls on responsive ears, but the flattery is built upon a partial truth.

Still, the principal impression which Bassiolo makes on us is of an absurd vanity which leads him to overreach his competence on nearly every possible occasion. It is possible that Chapman was lampooning some current court official whose identity is now lost, or even that he was satirizing the queen's lord chamberlain in the person of his deputy. That Chapman indulged in personal satire is evident from his lost *Old Joiner of Aldgate*, perhaps commissioned as a weapon in a current law case, from his share in *Eastward Ho*, and from the possibly suppressed scene involving the drunken Lady Furnifall in

13 Scott, *Sussex Archaeological Collections*, VII, 193; see *A Collection of Ordinances*, pp. 37–38, 109–110, *et passim*; Jones, pp. 155–156 *et passim*; Joseph Banks, ed., "Copy of an Original Manuscript, entitled 'A Breviate touching the Order and Governmente of a Nobleman's House, &c.'" (1605), *Archaeologia*, XIII (1800), 321–325. See also n. 17.

14 Chambers, I, 205.

APPENDIX C

Sir Giles Goosecap.[15] More likely, the satire is general and is directed to courtly behavior. The characterization of Bassiolo is not the only such treatment of household servants. In Dekker's *Guls Horne-Booke* (1609), the gentleman usher is taken as the type of courtly haughtiness: the young gallant is ironically advised to "walke up and downe . . . as scornfully and as carelesly [haughtily] as a Gentleman-Usher."[16] Prepasso, the gentleman usher in Marston's *Malcontent*, has a tiny role but a silly one; more obviously satirical of gentlemen ushers is the remark "she hated monkeys, fools, jesters, and gentlemen ushers" (*Malcontent*, V.ii.80–81); and Bilioso, who holds the similar office of marshall, is mercilessly ridiculed: he is duly obsequious to his master's changes of opinion about Malevole but is reprehensible as a human being and has, as his name implies, an excess of the choleric humor. In Chapman's *Tragedy of Chabot*, the Advocate's speech on the generative effects of corruption includes an uncomplimentary reference to gentlemen ushers, suggesting typical sexual and social impropriety: "The corruption of a captain may beget a gentleman-usher, and a gentleman-usher may beget a lord" (V.ii.29–31).

Finally, we may mention the portraits of Maffe, the steward in Chapman's *Bussy D'Ambois;* Argus and Clinias, who vie for the position of gentleman usher in Chapman's *Widow's Tears;* Oswald, Goneril's steward in *King Lear;* and Malvolio, the steward in *Twelfth Night* upon whom Bassiolo may have been partially modelled. Not all such servants in contemporary drama are ridiculous or evil: Flavius, the faithful steward in *Timon of Athens*, and Griffith, the queen's gentleman usher in *Henry VIII*, are not. Nonetheless, there seems to have been a marked tendency in the drama around and

---

[15] See Alfred Harbage, *Shakespeare and the Rival Tradition* (New York, 1952), p. 79. Although a connection between the name of Bassiolo and that of William Bas (or Basse) seems very unlikely, I mention the remote possibility. In 1602 Bas brought out a set of pastoral elegies and a poem called *Sword and Buckler, Or, Serving-Mans Defence;* little is known of Bas' life, but Anthony à Wood said that he was "sometime a retainer to the Lord [Richard] Wenman" of Oxfordshire (R. W. Bond, ed., *The Poetical Works of William Basse* [*1602–1653*] [London, 1893], p. xii). Bas said in his poem, however, that he was only a page because of his youth (stanza 73), and, although he later achieved some fame for a poem to Shakespeare's memory alluded to by Ben Jonson, he probably would not have been well enough known in 1602 or 1603 to warrant Chapman's satirizing him.

[16] *Elizabethan and Jacobean Pamphlets*, ed. George Saintsbury (London, 1892), p. 248.

shortly after 1600 to depict important household servants, particularly including gentlemen ushers, as somewhat less than admirable men whether they are admirable servants or not. This tendency is perhaps an outgrowth of the earlier tendency to depict servants as mere dolts, but it results in a rather more sophisticated and focused satire; for one thing, the specific offices held by servants in earlier plays were less often identified. The faults displayed in these household officers are not always the same, but the general conception in nearly all the works is in some way deprecatory. The deprecation, moreover, is not restricted to fictional works. We have a notable piece of advice conveyed by Henry Percy, Earl of Northumberland, to his son in 1609, in which, following an argument against uxoriousness, the earl warns:

> Gripe into yowr hands what poore [power] soe ever yow will of governement, yett will there be certain persons about yowr wyfe, that yow will never reduce;—a gentleman ushier, her tailor, and her woman; for they will ever talke, and ever be unreasonable; all whiche your officers will rather endeavour to pleas then yowr selfe, so as it be not a very mayne matter.[17]

Chapman's treatment of Bassiolo, then, appears to be consistent with a general attitude toward such officers at about the time when Chapman was writing.

[17] "Instructions by Henry Percy . . . to his Son Algernon Percy, Touching the Management of His Estate, Officers, &c. written during his Confinement in the Tower," ed. James H. Markland, *Archaeologia*, XXVII (1838), 337. Markland quoted a note by (Edmund?) Malone: "The Gentleman Usher constantly attended his mistress when she went abroad, and even went on messages to make inquiries concerning the health of her female friends. It should seem from what is here stated, that he was sometimes employed also by his mistress in *secret services*."

Appendix D

Theories of Revision

Parrott argued that the short first scene of Act III was a late addition, written to improve the exposition after a performance brought out "the inadequacy of the preparation for the plot against Strozza." He noted that the scene duplicates the brief conversation between Medice and the First Huntsman in III.ii.297–298 and theorized that, if III.i had been written first, "there would be no need whatever for the whispered colloquy of Medice with the Huntsman, nor for the latter's promise, since the murder would have already been arranged." After the scene was added, perhaps not by Chapman himself, he felt that lines 297–298 of Act III, scene ii, "were doubtless omitted in subsequent performances."[1] His argument is plausible and may be right,[2] but the duplication is not terribly disturbing: Medice could merely have been making sure. In any case, I doubt that the lines in III.ii were omitted from performance, for they provide the excuse for Medice and the First Huntsman to whisper onstage; as I have shown in the Introduction (n. 22), the staging, at that point, of three whispering groups represents the structure of conspiracy and counter-conspiracy upon which so much of the play hinges.

The other evidence which Parrott produced is in the time interval after III.i, which "takes place on the day preceding the events of the rest of Act III." According to Renaissance codification of classical rules, it would indeed have been more normal to have a time interval between acts rather than between scenes, and a playwright of Chap-

[1] T. M. Parrott, ed., *All Fooles and The Gentleman Usher by George Chapman*, The Belles-Lettres Series (Boston, 1907), pp. 287–288.

[2] He might also have noticed a discrepancy between III.i.2, which has Medice's claim that he has been "ever bountiful lord to thee," and I.i. 116–117, but such discrepancies are usually explainable by differences in speakers' attitudes, differences in dramatic situations, and the like. In III.i, the line gives the servant just enough motivation to make his agreement to murder seem reasonable.

man's tendencies might be expected to have obeyed the rules. But this is very tenuous evidence. The timing of the scene on the day before the hunt might have several explanations, or might require none at all; its situation in Act III is explainable, however, for Medice's plot is a counteraction, and the beginning of Act III was the normal place for it.

Akihiro Yamada has argued for much more extensive revisions, involving the whole play and stratifying the received text.[3] His arguments, however, are scarcely worth refutation, for they are based on trivia which have no significance to the question or even upon misinterpretations of the text. Revisions of particular lines there probably were, in the nature of things, and I have suspected that such revisions may have been made during a proofreading in the printshop; but I find no evidence of any thoroughgoing rewriting of the play.

[3] "Bibliographical Studies of George Chapman's *The Gentleman Usher* (1606) Printed by Valentine Simmes," *Shakespeare Studies* (Shakespeare Society of Japan), II (1963), 86–90; and the same author's unpublished Master's thesis, "An Edition of George Chapman's 'The Gentleman Vsher'" (Birmingham, 1962).

Appendix E

Chronology

Approximate years are indicated by *, occurrences in doubt by (?).

Political and Literary Events	*Life and Major Works of Chapman*

1558
Accession of Queen Elizabeth I
Robert Greene born.
Thomas Kyd born.

1560

George Chapman born in Hitchin in Hertfordshire.*

1561
Francis Bacon born.

1564
Shakespeare born.
Christopher Marlowe born.

1572
Thomas Dekker born.*
John Donne born.
Massacre of St. Bartholomew's Day.

1573
Ben Jonson born.*

1574
Thomas Heywood born.*

"Sent to the University" (probably Oxford, and later to Cambridge) "where he was observed to be most excellent in the Latin and Greek tongues" but "took no degree there" (Wood).*

1576
The Theatre, the first permanent public theater in London, established by James Burbage.
John Marston born.

1577
The Curtain theater opened.
Holinshed's *Chronicles of England, Scotland and Ireland.*
Drake begins circumnavigation of the earth; completed 1580.

1578
John Lyly's *Euphues: The Anatomy of Wit.*

1579
John Fletcher born.
Sir Thomas North's translation of Plutarch's *Lives.*

1580
Thomas Middleton born.

1583
Philip Massinger born.

1584
Francis Beaumont born.*

1586
Death of Sir Philip Sidney.
John Ford born.
Kyd's *THE SPANISH TRAGEDY.*

1587
The Rose theater opened by Henslowe.
Marlowe's *TAMBURLAINE,* Part I.*
Execution of Mary, Queen of Scots.
Drake raids Cadiz.

1588
Defeat of the Spanish Armada.
Marlowe's *TAMBURLAINE,* Part II.*

1589
Greene's *FRIAR BACON AND FRIAR BUNGAY.*
Marlowe's *THE JEW OF MALTA.*

1590
Spenser's *Faerie Queene* (Books I–III) published.

Sidney's *Arcadia* published.
Shakespeare's *HENRY VI*, Parts
I–III,* *TITUS ANDRONICUS.*

1591
Shakespeare's *RICHARD III.*

In Low Countries as member of
English Expeditionary Force (?).

1592
Marlowe's *DOCTOR FAUSTUS*
and *EDWARD II.*
Shakespeare's *TAMING OF THE
SHREW* and *THE COMEDY OF
ERRORS.*
Death of Greene.

1593
Shakespeare's *LOVE'S LABOR'S
LOST*;* *Venus and Adonis* published.
Death of Marlowe.
Theaters closed on account of
plague.

Associating with Raleigh, Roydon,
Marlowe, and Harriot in the
"School of Night."*

1594
Shakespeare's *TWO GENTLEMEN
OF VERONA*;* *The Rape of Lucrece*
published.
Shakespeare's company becomes
Lord Chamberlain's Men.
Death of Kyd.

The Shadow of the Night (*Hymnus in
Noctem* and *Hymnus in Cynthiam*).

1595
The Swan theater built.
Sidney's *Defense of Poesy* published.
Shakespeare's *ROMEO AND
JULIET,* *A MIDSUMMER
NIGHT'S DREAM,* *RICHARD
II.*
Raleigh's first expedition to Guiana.

*Ovid's Banquet of Sense, A Coronet for
His Mistress Philosophy, and His
Amorous Zodiac.*

1596
Spenser's *Faerie Queene* (Books
IV–VI) published.
Shakespeare's *MERCHANT OF
VENICE,* *KING JOHN.*
James Shirley born.

Chapman writing for the Admiral's
company.*
*THE BLIND BEGGAR OF ALEX-
ANDRIA* (printed 1598).
De Guina.

1597
Bacon's *Essays* (first edition).

AN HUMOROUS DAY'S MIRTH

Shakespeare's *HENRY IV*, Part I.*

(printed 1599), a prototype of the comedy of humors.

1598

Demolition of The Theatre.
Shakespeare's *MUCH ADO ABOUT NOTHING,* HENRY IV*, Part II.*
Jonson's *EVERY MAN IN HIS HUMOR* (first version).

Mentioned by Meres in *Palladis Tamia* as one of the best writers of comedy and tragedy.
Completes *Hero and Leander*; *Seven Books of the Iliads* (tr.); *Achilles Shield* (tr.).

1599

The Paul's Boys reopen their theater.
The Globe theater opened.
Shakespeare's *AS YOU LIKE IT,* HENRY V, JULIUS CAESAR.*
Dekker's *THE SHOEMAKERS' HOLIDAY.*
Marston's *ANTONIO AND MEL-LIDA,* Parts I and II.
Death of Spenser.

ALL FOOLS (printed 1605).

1600

Shakespeare's *TWELFTH NIGHT.*
The Fortune theater built by Alleyn.
The Children of the Chapel begin to play at the Blackfriars.

Begins writing for the recently revived children companies, Paul's Boys and the Children of the Chapel.

1601

Shakespeare's *HAMLET,* MERRY WIVES OF WINDSOR.*
Insurrection and execution of the Earl of Essex.
Jonson's *POETASTER.*

1602

Shakespeare's *TROILUS AND CRESSIDA.*

THE CONSPIRACY AND TRAGEDY OF CHARLES, DUKE OF BYRON (printed 1608); *SIR GILES GOOSECAP* (?)* (printed 1606).

1603

Death of Queen Elizabeth I; accession of James VI of Scotland as James I.

THE OLD JOINER OF ALDGATE (lost); *THE GENTLEMAN USHER* (printed 1606).

Florio's translation of Montaigne's *Essays* published.

Shakespeare's *ALL'S WELL THAT ENDS WELL.* *

Heywood's *A WOMAN KILLED WITH KINDNESS.*

Marston's *THE MALCONTENT.* *

Shakespeare's company becomes the King's Men.

1604

Shakespeare's *MEASURE FOR MEASURE,* * *OTHELLO.* *

Marston's *THE FAWN.* *

1605

Shakespeare's *KING LEAR.* *

Marston's *THE DUTCH COUR-TESAN.* *

Bacon's *Advancement of Learning* published.

The Gunpowder Plot.

1606

Shakespeare's *MACBETH.* *

Jonson's *VOLPONE.* *

Tourneur's *REVENGER'S TRAGEDY.* *

The Red Bull theater built.

Death of John Lyly.

1607

Shakespeare's *ANTONY AND CLEOPATRA.* *

Beaumont's *KNIGHT OF THE BURNING PESTLE.* *

Settlement of Jamestown, Virginia.

1608

Shakespeare's *CORIOLANUS,* * *TIMON OF ATHENS,* * *PERICLES.* *

Dekker's *Gull's Hornbook* published.

Richard Burbage leases Blackfriars theater for King's company.

John Milton born.

Becomes protege of Prince Henry, who appoints him his "sewer in ordinary" in 1604.

MONSIEUR D'OLIVE * (printed 1606); *BUSSY D'AMBOIS* * (printed 1607).

THE WIDOW'S TEARS * (printed 1612); *THE TRAGEDY OF CAESAR AND POMPEY* * (printed 1631).

EASTWARD HO, in collaboration with Jonson and Marston (printed 1605); Chapman and Jonson imprisoned because of alleged derogatory allusions to King James.

A spring performance of the *BYRON* plays with an indecorous presentation on the stage of the living French Queen results in vehement protests of the French Ambassador and to wholesale excisions in the printed text.

1609

Shakespeare's *CYMBELINE* ;*
SONNETS published.
Jonson's *EPICOENE*.

Euthymiae Raptus, or the Tears of
Peace; *Twelve Books of the Iliads* (tr.).
MAY DAY* (printed 1611).

1610

Jonson's *ALCHEMIST*.
Richard Crashaw born.

BUSSY D'AMBOIS revised* (printed 1641); *REVENGE OF BUSSY*
D'AMBOIS* (printed 1613).

1611

Authorized (King James) Version
of the Bible published.
Shakespeare's *THE WINTER'S*
TALE,* *THE TEMPEST*.*
Beaumont and Fletcher's *A KING*
AND NO KING.
Middleton's *A CHASTE MAID IN*
CHEAPSIDE.*
Tourneur's *ATHEIST'S*
TRAGEDY.*

The complete *Iliads* (tr.).

1612

Webster's *THE WHITE DEVIL*.*

Petrarch's Seven Penitential Psalms [tr.]
. . . *and a Hymn to Christ upon the*
Cross; *An Epicede, or Funeral Song*
(on the death on November 6 of
Prince Henry).
In subsequent years, without support
comparable to that from Prince
Henry, Chapman suffered financial
hardships.

1613

The Globe theater burned.
Shakespeare's *HENRY VIII* (with
Fletcher).
Webster's *THE DUCHESS OF*
MALFI.*
Sir Thomas Overbury murdered.

THE MASQUE OF THE MIDDLE
TEMPLE AND LINCOLN'S INN
(set designed by Inigo Jones), performed on February 15 as part of
the entertainment celebrating the
marriage of Princess Elizabeth to
Palsgrave, the Elector Palatine
(printed 1613).

1614

The Globe theater rebuilt.
The Hope theater built.
Jonson's *BARTHOLOMEW FAIR*.

Eugenia; *Andromeda Liberata, or The*
Nuptials of Perseus and Andromeda;
Justification of . . . *Andromeda Liberata*.

1615

The complete *Odysseys* (tr.).

1616
Publication of Folio edition of
Jonson's *Works*.
Death of Shakespeare.
Death of Beaumont.

The Whole Works of Homer (tr.);
Divine Poem of Musaeus (tr.).

1618
Outbreak of Thirty Years
War.
Execution of Raleigh.

Georgics of Hesiod (tr.).

1620
Settlement of Plymouth, Massachu-
setts.

1621–24.

*THE TRAGEDY OF CHABOT,
ADMIRAL OF FRANCE** (printed
1639).

1621
Middleton's *WOMEN BEWARE
WOMEN.**
Robert Burton's *Anatomy of
Melancholy* published.
Andrew Marvell born.

1622
Middleton and Rowley's *THE
CHANGELING.**
Henry Vaughan born.

Pro Vere, Autumni Lachrymae.

1623
Publication of Folio edition of
Shakespeare's *COMEDIES, HIS-
TORIES, AND TRAGEDIES.*

*An Invective . . . against Mr. Ben
Jonson.**

1624

Crown of All Homer's Works (tr.).*

1625
Death of King James I; accession
of Charles I.
Death of Fletcher.

1626
Death of Tourneur.
Death of Bacon.

1627
Death of Middleton.

1628
Ford's *THE LOVER'S MELAN-
CHOLY.*
Petition of Right.
Buckingham assassinated.
1629

Fifth Satire of Juvenal (tr.).

1631
Shirley's *THE TRAITOR*
Death of Donne.
John Dryden born.
1632
Massinger's *THE CITY MADAM.**
1633
Donne's *Poems* published.
Death of George Herbert.
1634
Death of Marston, Webster.*
Publication of *THE TWO NOBLE
KINSMEN*, with title-page attribu-
tion to Shakespeare and Fletcher.
Milton's *Comus.*

Chapman dies on May 12; buried
in the parish of St. Giles-in-the-
Fields, where Inigo Jones erects a
monument to his memory.

1635
Sir Thomas Browne's *Religio
Medici.*
1637
Death of Jonson.
1639
First Bishops' War.
Death of Carew.*
1640
Short Parliament.
Long Parliament inpeaches Laud.
Death of Massinger, Burton.
1641
Irish rebel.
Death of Heywood.

Revision of *BUSSY D'AMBOIS*
published.

1642
Charles I leaves London; Civil War
breaks out.
Shirley's *COURT SECRET.*

All theaters closed by Act of Parliament.

1643

Parliament swears to the Solemn League and Covenant.

1645

Ordinance for New Model Army enacted.

1646

End of First Civil War.

1647

Army occupies London.
Charles I forms alliance with Scots.
Publication of Folio edition of Beaumont and Fletcher's *COMEDIES AND TRAGEDIES*.

1648

Second Civil War.

1649

Execution of Charles I.

1650

Jeremy Collier born.

1651

Hobbes' *Leviathan* published.

1652

First Dutch War began (ended 1654).
Thomas Otway born.

1653

Nathaniel Lee born.*

1656

D'Avenant's *THE SIEGE OF RHODES* performed at Rutland House.

1657

John Dennis born.

1658

Death of Oliver Cromwell.
D'Avenant's *THE CRUELTY OF THE SPANIARDS IN PERU* performed at the Cockpit.

1660

Restoration of Charles II.

Theatrical patents granted to Thomas Killigrew and Sir William D'Avenant, authorizing them to form, respectively, the King's and the Duke of York's Companies.

1661

Cowley's *THE CUTTER OF COLEMAN STREET*.

D'Avenant's *THE SIEGE OF RHODES* (expanded to two parts).

1662

Charter granted to the Royal Society.

1663

Dryden's *THE WILD GALLANT*.

Tuke's *THE ADVENTURES OF FIVE HOURS*.

1664

Sir John Vanbrugh born.

Dryden's *THE RIVAL LADIES*.

Dryden and Howard's *THE INDIAN QUEEN*.

Etherege's *THE COMICAL REVENGE*.

1665

Second Dutch War began (ended 1667).

Great Plague.

Dryden's *THE INDIAN EMPEROR*.

Orrery's *MUSTAPHA*.

1666

Fire of London.

Death of James Shirley.